DATE DUE	
MAR 3 0 2013			

When the Nazis Came to Skokie

LANDMARK LAW CASES

AMERICAN SOCIETY

Peter Charles Hoffer
N. E. H. Hull
Series Editors

PHILIPPA STRUM

When the Nazis Came to Skokie

Freedom for Speech We Hate

1999

UNIVERSITY PRESS OF KANSAS

Published by the University Press of Kansas (Lawrence, Kansas 66049), which was
organized by the Kansas Board of Regents and is operated and funded by Emporia State
University, Fort Hays State University, Kansas State University, Pittsburg State
University, the University of Kansas, and Wichita State University.

Library of Congress Cataloging-in-Publication Data

Strum, Philippa.
When the Nazis came to Skokie : freedom for speech we hate /
Philippa Strum.
p.   cm. — (Landmark law cases & American society)
Includes bibliographical references and index.
ISBN 0-7006-0940-7 (cloth : alk. paper). — ISBN 0-7006-0941-5
(pbk. : alk. paper)
1. Freedom of speech—United States—Cases.   2. Assembly, Right
of—United States—Cases.   3. Skokie (Ill.)—Trials, litigation,
etc.   4. National Socialist Party of America—Trials, litigation,
etc.   5. Neo-Nazis—Illinois—Skokie.   6. Jews—Illinois—Skokie.
I. Title.   II. Series.
KF4772.A7S77   1999
342.73'0853—dc21   98-44613

British Library Cataloguing in Publication Data is available.

Printed in the United States of America

10 9 8 7 6 5 4 3 2 1

The paper used in this publication meets the minimum requirements
of the American National Standard for Permanence of Paper for
Printed Library Materials Z39.48-1984.

WITH THANKS TO THE WOODROW WILSON CENTER

AND ITS FELLOWS OF 1997–1998

CONTENTS

EDITORS' PREFACE

There are law cases whose resolution shines with moral truth—we know that they are rightly decided, and they become the benchmarks of later jurisprudence. One thinks of *Brown v. Board of Education* (1954). There are law cases whose resolution shakes the very foundations of our polity and imperils the legal regime. *Dred Scott v. Sanford* (1857) was one. As Philippa Strum demonstrates in this forcefully argued and thoroughly researched volume, there are cases just as important that do not have such resounding resolutions. A proposed rally of a handful of neo-Nazis in a suburb of Chicago that gave refuge to thousands of survivors of the Nazi concentration camps raised fundamental questions about freedom of political speech when that speech was intended to abuse and frighten an already abused minority.

Professor Strum's book is as much about the organization that defends basic constitutional principles like freedom of speech even when the beneficiaries of that defense may be less than admirable individuals. The American Civil Liberties Union has compiled an enviable record over the years since its founding in the first Red Scare era, but never were its public image and its sources of funding in greater danger than when it provided counsel for the neo-Nazis. How the ACLU weathered that storm is one of the most fascinating stories in this book.

Counsel for the town (and by proxy for the Holocaust survivors) argued with passion that freedom of speech doctrines did not protect "fighting words," slander, pornography, and hateful speech; but did the Nazis really pose a threat amounting to a clear and present danger to the survivors? The survivors in Skokie sought an injunction to bar the Nazis from wearing uniforms bearing swastikas, handing out leaflets, and marching. This amounted to a prior restraint of speech; but if the Nazis did not march, how could the survivors prove that they were harmed? Perhaps holding a counterdemonstration, or simply ignoring the Nazis, denying them the publicity they craved, was a better course? Strum handles all of these complex issues with clarity and balance.

Justice Oliver Wendell Holmes Jr. once wrote that hard cases make bad law. In the controversy over the Nazi presence in Skokie, all the elements for a hard case presented themselves. The clash of absolutes looked insoluble, but the purpose of courts and the job of counsel is to resolve disputes; the resolution of this dispute proved the professionalism and wisdom of the state and the federal courts. Yet the case itself and the logic of the decision remain hotly contested. Legal scholars have made *Skokie* a litmus test in debates over hate speech and Critical Race Theory. And there are those who still feel betrayed by the decision.

Professor Strum's account brings together finely delineated portraits of the protagonists and a brisk and learned analysis of the legal issues. Her fair-minded and thorough tracing of the lawyers' arguments demonstrates how seriously legal counsel take their jobs, even when they may be abused or misunderstood by the media and the public. In a cogent final section, Strum extends her analysis of the issues in Skokie to other hate speech issues and to international protections for political speech.

ACKNOWLEDGMENTS

Among the joys of book authorship are the people one meets during the process of research and writing. My warmest memories of *Skokie* are my meetings with Harvey Schwartz and Barbara O'Toole.

Judge Schwartz spent hours telling me stories of Skokie and showing me around the sites important to the story. I thank him for his time, his accessibility, and his willingness to share his recollections. Barbara O'Toole granted me access to her memories and analysis as well as to ACLU-Illinois files (for which thanks also go to Executive Director Jay Miller) and undertook to track down stray details. She also read through a draft of this volume. If she ever tires of the law, she has a career as an editor ahead of her.

My thanks go to a number of other interviewees and to helpful critics. Norman Dorsen shared his copious memory and his files, which contained information I could not have gotten elsewhere. Frank Haiman permitted me to interview him by telephone, read and commented copiously on a draft, and gave me the results of his own search for details. Of course his work on free speech was an inspiration.

Donald Downs permitted me to read his unpublished article, "Jews and the Law: the Skokie Free Speech Controversy," and corrected an early draft of this manuscript. H. N. Hirsch, the best of colleagues, sent me two of his then-unpublished articles about speech, and he too read and corrected an early draft.

I was fortunate to have other readers at various stages of this project, and my thanks go to David Goldberger and Michael Kahan for being among them. Two of my most faithful and constant if critical readers during recent years have been Jill Norgren and Melvin I. Urofsky. Jill meticulously went through a very rough first draft and covered it with copious and invaluable questions and comments. Mel performed the heroic feat of reading through two different drafts and suggesting a much-needed reorganization of the material. One could not ask for better or more generous reader-editors.

Amy Putnam, a superb research intern at the Woodrow Wilson Center, managed to make sense of my semiarticulate and unceasing demands for more information and took the initiative in finding material I hadn't known existed. Sarah Witt, librarian for the American Jewish Congress, was extremely helpful in locating files and making them accessible. Thanks also are due to the many librarians at the Library of Congress and the George Washington University law library who coped so well with incessant requests for what occasionally proved to be nonexistent materials. Zdenek David of the Woodrow Wilson Center library helped by keeping an eye out for reference works that he thought I might find useful.

Thanks are owed to Brooklyn College and to the City University of New York for the Scholar's Incentive grant that helped subsidize writing time.

My gratitude goes once again to Michael Briggs, editor-in-chief of the University Press of Kansas. I have revised my job description for editors as a result of knowing him, and I begin to wonder whether anyone else can fit the bill: intelligent, patient, generous, humorous, knowledgeable, and just plain nice. The opportunity to work with Susan Schott is one of the other delights of publishing with UPK, and Rebecca Knight Giusti was a whiz at mitigating the pains of readying the manuscript for publication.

The Woodrow Wilson Center quite literally made this volume possible. It would have been a far less substantial and a much longer project had I not been fortunate enough to recieve a 1997–1998 Fellowship at the center. There I experienced the gift of time and a community of scholar-fellows who combined their knowledge of disparate fields and their occasionally devastating queries with unfailing civility and encouragement. Their ability to home in on key questions about research in areas far from their own, during both our weekly work-in-progress sessions and more informal conversations, taught me a great deal about the ways in which good scholarship necessarily is a joint endeavor. The "class" of 1997–1998 was made up of special people.

The center is equally unique. I wish it could be cloned a hundredfold so that even more scholars could benefit from it. It is run by an incredibly helpful group of scholars who fully understand the rigors of research. I hope I will not hurt the feelings of some staffers by singling out Ann Sheffield, Ben Amini, Susan Nugent, Rositta Hickman, Marilyn Swann, Lindsay Collins, Arlyn Charles, and their various contributions to making work and life liveable. This volume is dedicated to the center, its staff, and my "classmates" of 1997–1998 as insufficient thanks for the important role played by the center in the endeavors of so many American scholars and others from all over the world.

Introduction

If there is any fixed star in our constitutional constellation, it is that no official, high or petty, can prescribe what shall be orthodox in politics, nationalism, religion, or other matters of opinion or force citizens to confess by word or act their faith therein.

JUSTICE ROBERT JACKSON, *West Virginia v. Barnette*, 1943

Francis Joseph Collin, known as Frank, called himself a Nazi. He believed that Jews and African Americans were biologically inferior and that the only way the United States could remain strong was to deprive Jews of citizenship and send all black Americans back to Africa. While he claimed not to advocate the immediate death of Jews, his idol was Adolf Hitler, the German Nazi leader who attempted to eradicate European Jews by having six million of them murdered in concentration camps during World War II.

Frank Collin wasn't German. He was an American, born in Illinois. He never traveled outside the United States. As do all Americans, he possessed inalienable rights, among them the right to believe and to speak in public about whatever obnoxious ideas he chose.

The place Collin and his two dozen uniformed followers chose to proclaim their Nazism in 1977, however, was the Chicago suburb of Skokie, the home of thousands of Holocaust survivors. These residents were among the minority of European Jews who had managed to escape death in Hitler's concentration camps and immigrate to the United States at the end of World War II. By 1977 they too were American citizens with inalienable rights. One of their rights, they believed, was to live peacefully and safely, dealing as best they could with their unspeakable memories of families brutally separated, of forced labor and starvation, and of those who were forced into gas chambers to die. They shuddered at the idea of American Nazis appearing in their town, wearing the same uniforms as the German Nazis who had enslaved them and killed their families. The psychological damage Collin's presence would inflict upon them gave *them* a right, they thought, that outweighed Collin's claim to parade his ideas in their village, and they were equally sure the American government would recognize that. So they went to court to keep Collin and his obnoxious ideas out of Skokie.

That was the background of a landmark case that caused many Americans to think about whether the right to speech ought to be as available to racists as it is to those whose rights are the racists' target. The First Amendment to the Constitution forbids government from making any law that would abridge the rights of free speech and assembly. Were there nonetheless limits to speech in the United States? Were there kinds of speech that were so out of bounds that they were not protected by the Constitution's First Amendment? Was potential psychological damage to people who had suffered enough sufficient reason to keep what the village of Skokie's lawyer called a "ragtag band" of Nazis from publicizing its ideas?

The questions were similar to those being asked about hate speech today, particularly hate speech on college and university campuses. And the way the drama of Skokie played itself out may suggest some answers.

Those of us who teach constitutional law refer to Skokie as a "classic" free speech case. To most members of the general public aware of the case, Skokie is the place where "the Nazis marched through a Jewish suburb." But there was no march through Skokie, and it wasn't a Jewish suburb. The media reported it as both, thereby indicating the way in which the media shapes the "facts" and raising a corollary question of just how much we really know about the issues that concern us all.

Similarly, the media has reported incidents of violation of campus speech codes such as a white male student calling some African-American women he thought were being overly loud outside his dormitory window "water buffalo." But the media has not drawn equal attention to instances of useful speech that was precluded by such codes. The case of a teaching assistant in psychology at the University of Michigan is an example. As a federal court reported, the university's speech code prevented him from raising in class the "hypothesis regarding sex differences in mental abilities . . . that men as a group do better than women in some spatially related mental tasks partly because of a biological difference." One might argue that having a set of rules on a university campus that criminalizes analysis of a theory is of questionable utility.

The reply might well be that speech in the classroom should not be covered by speech codes but speech outside the classroom should be covered. Fine—but what if a group of students goes to a professor's *office* for a discussion? What if student members of a seminar are invited to an end-of-semester party in the professor's home? Isn't the room in which they meet an extension of the classroom? Will the university now be permitted to regulate speech in someone's home? These are what constitutional experts call "slippery slope" questions: those that ask, "But where might your proposed action lead? Aren't you setting out on what could become a very slippery slope?"

When the venue is not a campus but a town and the question is about the asserted right of a group of Nazis to demonstrate on Holocaust survivors' streets, it is equally difficult to answer. Very few people would assert that causing survivors additional pain is a societal good. As it turned out, not too many more argued that free speech had to be protected because the cost of allowing the government to decide which speech is permissible is too high. But it was the second few who won in court. This volume explores the reasons and asks whether the outcome was a good thing for us all.

CHAPTER I

"We Are Coming"

*"[G]reat cases are called great . . . because of some accident of immediate overwhelming
interest which appeals to the feelings and distorts the judgment."*

JUSTICE OLIVER WENDELL HOLMES JR.,

DISSENTING IN *Northern Securities Co. v. United States* (1904)

Frank Collin was unlikely to win a contest for anyone's favorite person.
He seemed to revel in the knowledge of his unpopularity and the reasons
for it. Physically unprepossessing, Collin struck reporters as a posturing
little man. The *New York Times* described him as five feet, eight inches, 165
pounds, and "slightly paunchy." His thinning hair, cut to look like Hitler's,
was plastered across his scalp; his face was covered with razor nicks. He
claimed that he became a Nazi when he saw an anti-Nazi television program
called "The Twisted Cross," sponsored by the Jewish Anti-Defamation
League of B'nai B'rith. What impressed him most were the close-ups of
Hitler's face and the shots of the audience, whom Collin described as
"deeply moved as if they had just had an awakening to something very
important." "I saw a great man deeply committed to something very powerful," Collin would say later, adding, "I've loved Hitler ever since."

His conversion to Nazism was all the odder because Collin was half
Jewish. The FBI discovered that his birth certificate was made out in the
name "Frank Cohn." Stranger still, Collin was the son of a Holocaust survivor. His father, Max Cohn, was a Jew who had been imprisoned in the
concentration camp at Dachau, Germany, for three months. Cohn changed
his name to Collin in 1946, after he reached the United States, married
Virginia Hardyman, an American Catholic, and fathered Frank Cohn/
Collin. Max's work as a home furnishings dealer enabled the family to buy
a comfortable house in the Chicago suburb of Olympia Fields. It was there
that Frank and his three younger siblings grew up.

The family found Frank's Nazism incomprehensible and offensive. One
of Frank Collin's two sisters said in 1977 that she had not talked to her
brother "since I was 13." His maternal grandmother told reporters that while

Collin visited his family regularly, he was attached to his mother but "not friendly" with his father. The family, she added, completely disapproved of his Nazi activities.

Collin joined George Lincoln Rockwell's American Nazi Party in 1963 and soon moved to Arlington, Virginia, where he worked at the party's headquarters. Rockwell was assassinated in 1967 by another party member, and at the end of 1968 Collin left what by then was called the National Socialist White People's Party. He subsequently told the press that he broke with the party because it was ineffective and its officers were "scum." The party's story was that it threw Collin out when his birth certificate was released and that when he returned to Chicago he took some of the party funds with him. Whatever the reason, Collin later said that he began organizing the National Socialist Movement in Chicago on December 1, 1968. The group's name subsequently became National Socialist Party of America (NSPA). On April 16, 1970, Collin opened the party's headquarters in a small storefront dubbed "Rockwell Hall," at 2519 West 71 Street on Chicago's South Side. Collin resided upstairs with his German shepherd dog and two of his followers and made the NSPA his life.

The South Side was a hotbed of racial and ethnic tensions in 1977. Rockwell Hall was in the Marquette Park neighborhood, the home of first-or second-generation workers from Eastern Europe. Their neighborhood was almost all white, and they intended to keep it that way. Their "right" to decide who could live in the neighborhood was challenged by African Americans who were beginning to move into the Park area. Some of the local whites blamed Jewish landlords for the presence of blacks, claiming, "The Niggers are their fault." One of Collin's colleagues told columnist Bob Greene, "Negroes are far too stupid to accomplish things on their own. What we want to do is inform people that Jews are in control of everything in life." The community's response to its new residents was reflected in the graffiti scrawled on the side of Rockwell Hall: "Nigger Go Home." Collin meant that quite literally.

It was of course not advice that African Americans were about to accept, and in the summers of 1976 and 1977 the Martin Luther King, Jr. Coalition, a group of Chicago African Americans formed to resist racism in general and to confront Collin in particular, marched in Marquette Park. The Reverend Edgar Jackson spoke for the group: "We feel it as important for black men to walk freely through Marquette Park as it was for men to win the battle of Iwo Jima and Tripoli, or for James Meredith to win the battle to attend 'Ole Miss' and graduate, even though it took 20,000 American troops to assure him his rights." Reverend Jackson was referring to two crucial battles of World War II and to the first African American to attend the University of Mississippi. In the latter instance, the National Guard had to be mobilized to ensure that segregationists did not ignore a court order and keep Meredith off the campus.

The one hundred coalition members who marched in the park in July 1976 were met by brick-throwing white teenagers. In the ensuing melee, thirty-three people were injured and sixty-three were arrested, members of Collin's party among them. On another occasion when the coalition was marching with a permit, the police, who had been notified in advance, failed to show up in sufficient numbers to prevent violence. A few coalition members attempted to march nonetheless. White teenagers reacted by rioting, injuring several police officers. Chicago's political leaders, no champions of diversity, cheerfully turned color-blind when it came to groups outside the local Democratic Party machine that challenged the status quo. They would arrest any "troublemaker," black or white, although they managed to find an astonishing number of black "troublemakers." They decided that the trouble-makers in the coalition's march were the members of the coalition them-selves, and so the police arrested them rather than the whites who attacked them. One of the many ironies of the Skokie case is that however different the issue involved, it was precisely this kind of demonstration that Collin would attempt in Skokie and that the village would do its best to stop.

———

Skokie is approximately half an hour by car from Chicago. Its streets are lined with modest single-family houses and trees, interspersed with churches, synagogues, and parks. The red brick village hall, fronted by Corinthian columns and topped by a small gold dome, was built in 1927. In 1977 it was surrounded by grass, and to enter it one walked a short paved path and then up the small flight of steps leading to the front door. The hall, at 5127 Oakton Street, was in the downtown business district and in sight of a few large condo buildings. With a population of 70,000, Skokie was large enough to be labeled a small city, but it liked to call itself "The World's Largest Village," and its atmosphere was indeed more like that of a bustling village.

Skokie, originally called Niles Centre, was populated in the mid–nineteenth century by immigrants from Germany, and up until the second World War it was common to hear German spoken there. A Skokie resident recalled that between 1937 and 1941 members of the Chicago German-American Volksbund, wearing their Nazi uniforms, occasionally paraded down one of Skokie's main streets. Their demonstrations would end when they reached Otto Decker's restaurant, the one with the big picture of Adolf Hitler. There, they engaged in close-order drills and speeches before retiring to the bar. By the summer of 1941, however, with the American media carrying stories of Hitler's troops rampaging through Europe and the American military draft in place, the Nazis had stopped marching in Skokie.

After the war, Skokie became something of a middle-class bedroom community for Chicago. Residents with rising incomes were able to move further away from Chicago, and many of their homes were sold to Jews: both American-born Jews, large numbers of them moving out of the inner-city Chicago neighborhoods that were increasingly populated by African Americans, and hundreds of Jewish death-camp survivors and their families. Skokie's first known Jewish religious service was held in the village hall in 1952, there not yet being a synagogue in the village.

There is no official population register by religious affiliation in the United States, so it is difficult to know exactly how many of Skokie's 70,000 residents were Jewish or to pinpoint the number of them who were survivors. *Chicago Tribune* reporter Jack Mabley counted 26 houses of worship in 1977: "1 Baptist, 3 Lutheran, 3 Catholic, 1 North Shore Assembly of God, 2 Presbyterian, 1 Bible church, 1 Christian Scientist, 1 Suburban Christian, 1 Methodist, 1 Baha'i, 1 Episcopal, 1 United Church of Christ," and 9 synagogues (others set the figure at 7). Different estimates of the proportion of Jews among Skokie's residents were offered as the case was heard in the courts. Marvin Bailey, the village's director of housing development, guessed that approximately 30,000 were Jewish, 5,000 to 6,000 of them survivors and their families. The opinions of various courts referred to 40,500 Jews, including 7,000 survivors and families. Those numbers were taken from a brief filed by village counsel Harvey Schwartz, who revised his estimate to 30,000 Jews years after the case was over. Assistant village counsel Gilbert Gordon thought in 1977 that the figure was 40 percent, or 28,000. All of the numbers were no more than educated guesses. The important point was that a large proportion of Skokie's population was Jewish and that it included a substantial number of Holocaust survivors.

There had been overt racism in Skokie before 1977. Donald Perille, chairman of the Skokie Plan Commission, remembered hundreds of "for sale" signs going up after the first black family moved to Skokie in 1961, and some violence as well. One day in the late 1960s law enforcement officials told the village government that George Lincoln Rockwell had threatened to visit Skokie during the Jewish High Holy Days, wearing full Nazi uniform and parading in front of a synagogue. Village officials called all the rabbis together to inform them of the possible appearance and to work out a strategy. The rabbis were unfazed. Then as now, so many American Jews who didn't otherwise attend synagogue wanted to worship during the High Holy Days that synagogues and temples had taken to issuing admission tickets, largely to assure seats for the regular members of their congregations. One Skokie rabbi's jocular response to the Rockwell threat was, "Well, he can come to Skokie but he'll never get into my synagogue without a ticket." There was no talk about "throwing up the barriers," Harvey Schwartz recalled; it was generally agreed that the best policy was to ignore Nazis and deprive them of the publicity they craved.

By 1977, the situation in Skokie had changed. Most of the survivors had lived a self-contained life, avoiding discussing their experiences with their neighbors. Perhaps they thought no one else would understand and were afraid of a negative response to the stories; perhaps they could not yet bring themselves to speak of their horrendous trauma. But by 1977, thanks in part to Mayor Albert J. Smith, a Catholic Notre Dame graduate who had read widely about the Holocaust and who considered the survivors to be his special charge, they had become a political force and were ready to speak out.

One of their most important leaders was a man named Sol Goldstein.

———

Goldstein, a manufacturer of dental materials, was remembered by those who knew him as magnetic, charismatic, and "like steel, tested beyond limits." He was a small man with a big belly and a thick accent. The years that he could never forget, however, were those when his belly was unnaturally shriveled.

Goldstein was born in Minsk, part of Czarist Russia, on March 30, 1914. His family soon moved to the Lithuanian city of Kovno. There he graduated from the University of Lithuania with a degree in chemical engineering. He married in 1941, when he was twenty-seven, by which time he already owned his home. The cosmopolitan Jewish community of which the Goldsteins were a part had created a hospital, an orphanage, a home for the aged, restaurants, community centers, schools, a clinic, a bank, and four newspapers. Most of its 30,000 to 35,000 members, some of whom had been educated in England or the United States, were professionals, merchants, clerks, craftsmen. About 6,000 of Kovno's poorer Jews lived in dilapidated wooden one-story houses in the suburb of Vilijampole, across the Vilija River, which had been a Jewish village for four centuries.

Hitler's plan for Europe included the isolation and, eventually, the destruction of Jewry. The most obvious signal was given by his followers on November 9, 1938, in what became known as "Kristallnacht," or "Glass Night." Thousands of Jews already had been forcibly deported from Germany to Poland. In reaction, a young German Jew killed an official of the German embassy in Paris. That night, with the Nazis' blessing, many Germans went on a rampage, smashing windows and destroying almost all of Germany's six hundred synagogues as well as thousands of Jewish homes and businesses. Hundreds of Jews were killed; tens of thousands more were arrested, ultimately to be put into concentration camps. A decree immediately transferred all Jewish-owned businesses in Germany to "Aryan" (non-Jewish white) control. "Concentration camps" actually were death camps whose names became infamous for the large number of Jews, Romany gypsies, political enemies of Nazism, homosexuals, and Jehovah's Witnesses who were killed there: Auschwitz, Bergen-Belsen, Buchenwald, Dachau, Maidenek, Treblinka. Many of the six million Jews who died in them came from Eastern and Western Europe, which were rapidly occupied by the German Army in the years immediately following Kristallnacht.

On June 22, 1941, the people of Kovno, Sol Goldstein among them, learned from their radios that Lithuania's war with Nazi Germany had begun. Military planes suddenly were flying above the city. The population panicked, and Goldstein thought that he and his new wife should flee. But June 22 was a Sunday, the banks were closed, and the Goldsteins wanted to have their savings as they faced an unknown future. All that night German bombs rained on Kovno. Early Monday morning Goldstein and many other Kovno Jews were in line in front of his bank, waiting anxiously for its business day to begin. When the doors opened at 10 A.M., however, it was only to disgorge an official who announced that the bank was closed for an indefinite period. Goldstein immediately began walking out of town to the east, but it was too late: the German Army had arrived. Messerschmitt airplanes were strafing people fleeing from Kovno, and German bombs were destroying the roads. Mass murder of Jews was taking place in nearby villages.

Returning to Kovno, Goldstein learned that his home already had been taken over by non-Jews and that many Jewish men had been arrested during the night. Several hundred others had been killed by organized Lithuanian gangs, anti-Semitism having had a long if less than honorable history in Lithuania. "Stores were closed," he remembered; "food was impossible to get." Only those Jews who could not help it left the comparative safety of their homes, as they were liable to be beaten by roving mobs or arrested. Home was not necessarily a refuge, however, as Lithuanian gangs surrounded apartment buildings, drove the occupants whom they didn't murder or rape outside at gunpoint, and looted their apartments. On June 25, a thousand Jews were killed by Nazi-backed Lithuanian mobs; many of them were burned to death in their wooden homes in Vilijampole. On June 27, sixty Jews were taken to a garage in the city center and, with a crowd watching, were either beaten to death with iron bats or killed by car-wash hoses that were crammed into their mouths and turned on full force. The jails, and the outer-city forts that were pressed into service as prisons, were filled to bursting with thousands of Jews, including 3,000 women and children. The younger and prettier women were raped, tortured, and then murdered by Lithuanian guards and their friends. The Lithuanians called it "going to peel potatoes." On July 6, 1,800 Jews were killed at one of the forts. six thousand Jewish men were imprisoned in another fort and never emerged.

The Jews of Kovno quickly became familiar with the different uniforms worn by the Nazis. Many of the Germans were members of the Sturmabteilung, or SA, which made decisions about the fate of the ghetto and its residents. Goldstein never forgot their tall boots and their brown uniforms with a swastika on the left arm, a swastika on the hat, and another swastika on the left chest of the yellow shirt. The uniforms differentiated them from members of the Schutzstaffel (SS), a group originally organized as Hitler's bodyguards and later assigned to carry out the murder of the European Jews. They too wore boots and had swastikas on their uniforms. Their shirts were black and their hats bore a picture of a skull. Frank Collin and his friends would model their uniforms after the SA's.

On July 10 the Nazis announced that the entire Jewish population of Kovno would be moved across the river to Vilijampole, whose 6,000 Jews were also interned but whose 2,000 non-Jewish inhabitants were ordered out and encouraged to move into the houses forcibly vacated by the Kovno Jews. Guard towers were quickly erected on the perimeter of the ghetto and manned by Nazis with machine guns. The Jews were ordered to wear

{ *When the Nazis Came to Skokie* }

a yellow Star of David on the front of their clothing, to build a barbed-wire fence around the new ghetto, to venture outside it only between 6 A.M. and 8 P.M. The Nazis imposed other restrictions: Jews needed new identity cards to show that they were gainfully employed and to claim food rations. Men were made to wear hats, which they had to remove obsequiously whenever a German came into sight. (After a Lithuanian policeman killed one Jewish man with his hat on, ghetto residents were quick to remove them in the presence of any non-Jew.) On July 28 they were forbidden to walk on sidewalks rather than in a single file in the gutter, enter parks or the beaches along the river, or use public transport. Three days later all their property was confiscated. Various decrees issued throughout August forbade them to shop in public markets except during specified hours, when most of the shelves had already been swept bare; to walk on the shores of the river or with their hands in their pockets; to bring food or newspapers into the ghetto; to keep electrical stoves and ovens rather than turn them over to the Nazis. On August 18, Goldstein remembered, Nazi officers came to the ghetto and asked for "501 college graduates, intellectuals, for special work for the German authorities, men only." Ghetto residents were so desperate by then that 534 men lined up, hoping for intellectual work and better food. They were led away, and the one or two who escaped subsequently returned to the ghetto to report that all the others had been killed at one of the forts. In September Jews were prohibited from buying food outside the ghetto and were ordered to turn over all valuable metals, paintings, carpets, pianos, typewriters, horses, cows, poultry, and material for suits and coats. In October the infectious-disease hospital and orphanage were cordoned off by the Nazis and set ablaze, their occupants still inside.

Goldstein remembered when a hundred or so men were herded into a garage by the Nazis, covered with gasoline, and set aflame. Somewhat later a number of elderly women were locked into an abandoned school building. After a week without food or water, they were taken out and thrown alive into a well that was then covered with dirt and gravel. Goldstein's mother was one of the women left there to smother to death.

On October 28 the remaining ghetto residents were ordered to line up by families at 6 A.M.—ironically enough, in a locale called Democracy Square, now surrounded by machine-gun emplacements. Anyone found at home would be shot. The local SA leader arrived and began separating people to left and right, breaking up families in the process. There were old people barely able to stand, crying children, husbands and wives desperately trying to maintain sight of each other. As the day wore on some of the elderly who had been standing for hours crumpled to the ground and died. It was announced that the Germans wanted to split up the ghetto and that the new group would go to different ones. When the process ended at the end of the day, according to Goldstein's estimate, 13,000 had been sent to the right and 15,000 to the left. At night the 13,000 (other survivor accounts put the number at 10,000) were marched off, with only a few escapees making it back to the ghetto the next morning. Everyone in their group had been told to undress and hand over their belongings, and then they were shot. The Nazis brought much of the seized clothing to the ghetto for use by those who remained. Wearing their dead neighbors' clothes as their own fell apart, the surviving Jews became forced laborers for the Nazis. Each morning they were marched outside the ghetto in squadrons to perform whatever hard labor had to be done or sent to the clothing and shoe workshops set up inside. Those who did not die or were not deported to death camps would be kept in the ghetto for three years.

In September 1942, in what was called the "Children's Action," the SA ordered all children under eleven or twelve to be separated from their parents. The skeptical Jews were told that the children would be better off in an area designated just for them. "Mothers came whose infant they grabbed from her arms, the children, the infants," Goldstein recalled, and then the Nazis "threw them—threw them in the vans like packages and took them away, and this was the Children's Action, and they killed them, too."

The winter of 1941 was a particularly cold one. Many people dismantled wooden outhouses for firewood; the cesspools overflowed, their contents frozen into icebergs of filth. Hunger was rampant. In the spring the ghetto residents dug new cesspools and built a public bathhouse in their attempt to keep clean and to ward off disease. The living space allotted to each person was gradually limited to three square feet, the crowding ensuring that all illnesses were shared. Then, in the summer and fall of 1942, thousands of wounded German Army officers were transferred from the eastern front to Kovno. Ghetto workers were forced to delouse them and disinfect their clothes, as many were infected with typhus. Some of the workers inevitably caught the disease. With the Nazis' murder of the infectious-disease hospital's patients, doctors, and nurses all too vivid in their minds, the ghetto residents were at pains to hide anyone who became ill with typhus. A heroic ghetto doctor worked feverishly to contain the epidemic, training families to care for patients, smuggling extra food to them, and moving children to other homes. With no medication available, he somehow managed to save 95 percent of those infected.

Goldstein and his wife escaped from the ghetto in October 1942. They joined the partisans who were waging guerrilla warfare on the Nazis, always on the edge of starvation and frequently dying from malnutrition and illness. Goldstein's wife was one of those who died. Somehow Goldstein survived. He arrived in the United States in 1948 and became a resident of Skokie, where Frank Collin and his band of Nazis chose to demonstrate.

Collin did not experience much of World War II or its impact on the American people and economy. He was born in 1945, when the war was drawing to a close. He thought he was carrying on the Nazi ideal, however, and he dressed himself and his followers in complete Nazi regalia. He would describe it in court: "We wear brown shirts with a dark brown tie, a swastika pin on the tie, a leather shoulder strap, a black belt with buckle, dark brown trousers, black engineer boots, and either a steel helmet or a cloth cap . . . plus a swastika arm band on the left arm and an American flag patch on the right arm." Their boots went up to their knees. They frequently carried red, white, and black flags, which also bore the swastika. Collin himself wore several more swastikas, including one on his belt buckle. Mike Royko, a *Chicago Daily News* columnist, saw him as a "dippy Nazi" and a "warped twerp." But the little man terrified the Skokie survivors as much as another "little man," Adolf Hitler, had terrified them back in Europe.

The NSPA's official program had thirty points. Among them were

I. Final solution of the Jewish Question through documented exposure of the destructive effect of Jewry on American society and Western Civilization.

II. Awarding of citizenship only to those 18 year old Americans of Aryan descent.

III. A National Eugenics Commission for . . . the elimination of all racial impurities.

IV. Prosecution of all individuals guilty of race-mixing activities.

VIII. Liquidation of all Zionist, pro-Zionist and other treasonous organizations.

Carrying on the theme of racial "purity," the program also called for "repatriation of all American Negroes to their African homeland" and "abolition of the pro-Communist, race-mixed United Nations." The party claimed to be against pollution, narcotics peddlers, degenerate arts, the federal income tax, the Federal Reserve System, unemployment, gangsterism, and crime. It supported public execution of all "convicted rioters and looters" and "convicted narcotics peddlers," preservation of the "Free Enterprize [*sic*] System and the rights of private property," "Reunification of the family as the hub of society," and "An authoritarian form of republic government founded on the ideals originally expressed in the United States Constitution." One of its flyers quoted extensively from Abraham Lincoln, with emphasis on the prepresidential speeches in which he spoke of racial equality as an impossible goal. The flyer publicized the NSPA's "Lincoln Plan," named by the NSPA after Abraham Lincoln and George Lincoln Rockwell, which would take money from foreign aid, welfare, and "bureaucratic swindles" and give it to "our own Negroes to establish their own nation with all the modern industries and conveniences of American life."

Collin testified in court that "[B]asically we believe that the Jews are in the forefront of the international Communist revolution and that they have inordinate amounts of political and financial power in the United States and throughout the world." Asked if he thought American Jews should be exterminated, he replied, "No." His solution was to expose and document "Jewish involvement in Communism and in the Federal Reserve conspiracy," presenting the evidence "to the American public for their own conclusions." He told the *Chicago Tribune,*

> Our aim is to establish an all-white America.
>
> First, we must take steps to put us in political power constitutionally, the same way the Democrats and Republicans win power.
>
> Then we must use that power legally, through a constitutional convention, to pass amendments restricting citizenship. To be a citizen, you would have to be a member of the race.

That was the platform on which Collin proposed to demonstrate, not at first in Skokie, but in Chicago.

––––––

The Martin Luther King, Jr. Coalition was not the only group to have marched in Chicago's Marquette Park; so had Collin and his followers. After the violence that followed the coalition's demonstration in the summer of 1976, the Chicago Park District "discovered" that any group wishing to march in the park had to post between $100,000 and $300,000 in public liability insurance and a $50,000 bond against property damage—a total the district estimated at $250,000. That negated the efforts of both the coalition and the NSPA, neither of which had access to anything even close to $250,000. Collin called the Illinois affiliate of the American Civil Liberties Union, which began a suit in federal court against the park district, claiming that the insurance requirement constituted an unconstitutional restriction on freedom of speech and assembly. The ACLU also had discussions with the King Coalition about possible representation, but the coalition was uncomfortable about using an organization that represented Nazis.

Collin, with a small following and an even smaller budget, knew that the only way he could get attention was through media coverage of his demonstrations. Now Chicago was making that impossible. Frustrated, he decided in September 1976 to embark on a new project in about a dozen suburbs to the north of Chicago. Collin knew that a good number of Jews lived in each of them. The leaflets he had distributed by the thousands carried a headline screaming, "WE ARE COMING!" and bore a caricature of a swastika reaching out to throttle a stereotyped Eastern European ghetto Jew. The Anti-Defamation League, a national Jewish organization with a Midwest office in Chicago, began to receive complaints and expressions of fear from North Shore Jews. Bob Greene of the *Chicago Sun-Times* thereupon interviewed Collin and took Collin's message to the large number of *Sun-Times* readers. Collin had happily revealed to Greene his purpose of gaining supporters while threatening Jewish inhabitants. The leaflet had read in part, "Where one finds the most Jews, there one will find the most Jew haters." Now Collin added, "We want to reach the good people—get the fierce anti-Semites who have to live among the Jews to come out of the woodwork and stand up for themselves." He had every intention of frightening Holocaust survivors who saw the leaflets: "I hope they're terrified. I hope they're shocked. Because we're coming to get them again. I don't care if someone's mother or father or brother died in the gas chambers. The unfortunate thing is not that there were six million Jews who died. The unfortunate thing is that there were so many Jewish survivors."

That publicity didn't satisfy Collin. He followed up in October 1976 by sending letters to the park districts of the North Shore suburbs, asking for permits to demonstrate for white power. The letters were typed on the NSPA stationery that carried a large swastika across the top. They were ignored by every suburb that received them—except for Skokie.

———

Collin's letter asked each suburb to issue a permit for a rally by the NSPA. In the case of Skokie, it was to be held on the steps of the village hall. No local government has an obligation to permit the use of any particular public place for meetings and demonstrations; but where such permission is granted to one group, the municipality must grant it to all others that are equally willing to meet criteria such as notice to the appropriate governmental officials and scheduling at a time when other groups are not already scheduled. Control of public space through the issuance of permits is designed both to maintain order and to enable citizens to exercise their rights to speak, join with others who have similar ideas, and assemble. So Collin, no stranger to demonstrations, knew that he had to acquire a permit.

His letter went to the Skokie Park District, which grants such permits. The park district is technically separate from the village government. Mayor Smith was unaware that the letter had been received or that the reply of the district's trustees, sent to Collin on October 25, 1976, said that the NSPA would have to post a bond for $350,000 in order to hold the demonstration. It was a requirement that the park district, surprised that there seemed to be no local ordinance enabling it to ban the demonstration, had adopted as soon as it received Collin's letter. The NSPA of course had no such amount in its coffers, and as the courts ascertained subsequently, no insurance company would provide it with that amount of money.

The new regulation played right into Collin's hands. Now he could claim that because the insurance requirement was so high, he was being kept from demonstrating in violation of his constitutional rights. On March 20, 1977, he wrote to Chief of Police Kenneth B. Chamberlain, announcing that the NSPA would demonstrate in Skokie on May 1. "Our intentions," Collin wrote, "are to protest the Skokie Park District's un-Constitutional request that we supply the District with $350,000.00 worth of insurance per rally." He made the demonstration sound as innocuous as possible: it would take place on the sidewalks outside the village hall rather than on the streets and would not interfere with pedestrian or automobile traffic, it would last no more than thirty minutes, and the group would "abide by all town ordinances." Collin added, "It has been our experience with the

Chicago Police Department to mutually lay down informal 'ground rules' both sides may work through before our public demonstrations. I am at your disposal for similar discussions." The police chief was opening his letter at the same time park district officials were reading another one from Collin, detailing the intended demonstration. It would take place in front of the village hall on Sunday, May 1, at 3 P.M., for about thirty minutes. Between thirty and fifty members of NSPA were expected to participate. (In his letter to Chamberlain, Collin gave the number as no more than two hundred. That, however, was boasting; he had never been able to muster so large a demonstration.) Maintaining his posture as a victim whose right to free speech was under attack by the village of Skokie, Collin said his followers would carry signs proclaiming, "White Free Speech," "Free Speech for White Americans," and "Free Speech for the White Man."

Now the park district did inform Mayor Smith and village counsel Harvey Schwartz. Their reaction was that for better or worse the law was clear: the First Amendment protected Collin's group, despicable as it was. Skokie had lived through demonstrations or threatened demonstrations in the past and would do so again. No one expected it to become a major problem rather than a passing annoyance.

Fred Richter was president of the Synagogue Council of the Northwest Suburbs, which by his estimate represented nine thousand to ten thousand of Skokie's Jews. Learning about Collin's plan in mid-March, he promptly called a meeting of the council for March 30. It was decided there that council officials would request additional information from the Skokie government. Mayor Smith, aware both of the council's concern and of his own responsibility to see that the proposed demonstration did not become a problem, convened an April meeting of the local rabbis and some local Jewish leaders. Chicago representatives of the Anti-Defamation League (ADL) were also invited because of the large Jewish organization's record of fighting anti-Semitism. The ADL routinely urged localities faced with an impending demonstration to adopt a "quarantine" policy, permitting and ignoring the demonstration in order to deprive the demonstrators of the publicity they sought. It was unanimously decided at the meeting called by Smith that this tactic would be followed, with the understanding that the rabbis would inform their congregations about the matter and the quarantine policy. That, the Skokie officials thought, would be that.

It wasn't. Each rabbi spoke to his congregation about the demonstration, explaining the quarantine policy. Each found himself facing congregation members who stood up to oppose it. Abbot Rosen, the Anti-Defamation League's Midwest leader and an ACLU member, told Skokie audiences that any attempts to block the demonstration would only give the Nazis the publicity they craved. "The less publicity you give these clowns the less likely they are to grow," he counseled. The strongly negative reaction he got from Jewish audiences surprised him. As long as the ADL maintained its traditional position, he later said, its popularity in the Jewish community plummeted.

On April 21, Fred Richter held another meeting of the Synagogue Council, inviting representatives of Jewish organizations in Skokie as well as Chicago-based Jewish organizations. About fifteen to eighteen such groups attended, as did representatives of national Jewish groups. Rejecting a suggestion that everyone simply stay away from the village hall for the demonstration's half hour—the quarantine policy—the meeting adopted a resolution to oppose the march and to stage a counterdemonstration a few blocks from the hall on the morning of May 1. Flyers began to appear in Skokie. Some apparently were produced by a coalition of left-wing organizations in Chicago that was planning its own counter-demonstration. Others may have been distributed by the NSPA. One of the latter, headlined "Smash the Jewish System" and bearing a crude caricature of a Jew and a swastika, claimed that the swastika was a symbol of "total resistance against the niggerization of our country." It also told readers that a "beautiful, full-color poster" was being prepared. "The poster shows three rabbis involved in the ritual murder of an innocent Gentile boy during the hate-fest of Purim. Our propaganda will deal at large with revealing quotes, many never before presented anywhere, from loose-lipped Hebes. In short, our successful opposition to the Black invasion of Southwest Chicago will now be turned on the culprits who started it all: the Jews!" Some Jewish residents reported abusive telephone calls in the early hours of the morning. Goldstein had in fact complained about threatening phone calls early in March, and the police chief had told the village government that Skokie residents were getting "the highest volume of this type of call that we have ever received." And now the Holocaust survivors began to speak out.

Goldstein became the best known of the Skokie survivors. Another of their leaders was Erma Gans. She had survived the experience of being sent to die in Auschwitz. Most of the rest of her family were less lucky and perished. "You could see the abilities that made her a survivor," village attorney Harvey Schwartz recalled. She struck him as remarkably strong and able. When she reached the United States, Gans went to college and did graduate work in sociology at Chicago's Loyola University. She and her survivor husband ran a successful printing business in a suburb west of Skokie. Gans had helped organize and was president of the Korzcak Lodge, Skokie's major formal association of survivors. She had run unsuccessfully for state office and spoke widely about the Holocaust at public events. Thinking about Gans and the other Skokie survivors, Schwartz ruminated, "These were people who never lost a struggle. If there was only so much to eat or wear or drink, they got it. I wasn't there—how do I know this? I don't have any facts—but they survived." It was survivors like Goldstein and Gans who got up at worship services and community meetings and declared that they were absolutely opposed to the Nazis being allowed to march in Skokie.

Throughout April, Mayor Smith and village attorney Schwartz had been appearing together to explain the way the village government proposed to react to the planned demonstration. They had no doubt that the quarantine policy should be followed for both legal and political reasons. "We had a good legal staff," Schwartz said. "Our research was along traditional lines in terms of what we felt were the First Amendment principles" of free speech and assembly. Ignoring the demonstration also was "the smart thing to do" from the standpoint of denying the Nazis publicity. As May 1 approached, the two men, accompanied by village council members, went to one such meeting at the Skokie Central Traditional Synagogue. Schwartz knew that Smith agreed with the position they had decided upon. But he also wondered whether Smith would maintain it.

Smith had read extensively about the Holocaust, finding it so shocking and repulsive that he had referred to it in many of the speeches he had made in his six years as mayor. As a result, he was regularly called upon as a speaker for Israel Bonds' fund-raising campaigns. The Skokie survivors regarded him as something of a miracle: a non-Jew who was totally in sympathy with them and committed to their causes. In a village dominated by the Democratic Party, to which most of Skokie's Jews belonged, Smith always ran for office under the nonpartisan Caucus label and always won. He had the solid support of the Jewish community and easily beat the occasional prominent Jewish Democrat who ventured to run against him. While Smith knew the law of the First Amendment, he also came as close as possible to understanding the survivors' pain.

A crucial moment for Smith may have come at a public meeting shortly after the arrival of Collin's March 20 letter. There, Smith was approached by a survivor who recounted the experience of watching his two-year-old daughter die when a Nazi prison guard smashed her head with his rifle butt. The survivor begged the mayor to understand the distress the sight of Nazi uniforms would cause him, his strong need to take action, and his inability to promise not to react violently. That was the attitude of the survivors who spoke at the meetings: having lived quietly with their agonizing memories, they now chose to stand up and fight. They could not permit Nazi uniforms on the streets of their home town.

Many of the village officials, including those who were Jewish, were hearing from the survivors for the first time. The Jewish survivor community and the rest of the Jewish community had lived side by side in Skokie without the latter knowing any more about the survivors' experiences and fears than did most Americans. The survivors had not discussed with their fellow citizens the horrors they had lived through. Many had even hesitated to speak about the Holocaust with their children, in part to spare the next generation the awful knowledge and in part because it was unspeakable. For the most part, they wanted to bury the past rather than bear verbal witness to it.

But now, perhaps in part because they had lived in "safe" small communities before the Holocaust and were living in a safe small community once again, they felt that this time they had to stop their community from being invaded. They felt guilty at having survived when so many others had not and at not having made what almost certainly would have been futile attempts to save others ahead of themselves. They were alive, which meant to them that they had not resisted hard enough: if they had, they would be dead, but perhaps those who had perished would still be alive. Now they had a chance to atone, to assuage a guilt that was no less painful for being unrealistic, to take the kind of action that had been impossible for them in the 1940s but that they nonetheless blamed themselves for not having taken. As far as the officials could tell, the survivors had no fear of imminent physical danger from the Nazis. "It was much, much more complex and deeper and personal," Schwartz knew, and added, "I think reliving the experience made it possible for them to unburden themselves about many things that had occurred in their past. . . . There had to be a lot of catharsis in that experience."

One survivor, described by the *Chicago Tribune* as a "soft-spoken grandmother" whose parents and brother had been killed in the Warsaw ghetto, told a reporter, "Years ago, in Europe, when the Nazis marched, we stayed in our houses, afraid. Now I am not afraid. I want to face them. What can they do to me now? This time they won't put us in gas chambers." A member of the Warsaw Ghetto Uprising drew on the behavior of Jews in Europe during the Holocaust when she said, "We will not cower in the high school while 100 notables speak for us."

The survivors were bewildered by the village government's response to Collin's proposed demonstration. This was the United States, not Nazi Germany, or Lithuania or Poland under the Nazis: wasn't the government supposed to protect *them?* Wasn't it the job of a democratically elected government to safeguard their right not to have to relive unspeakable horrors?

The meeting at the Central Synagogue was filled with political supporters and friends of the mayor, many of them survivors. Smith was startled as one survivor after another got up to say that they opposed the plan: the Nazis could not be permitted in Skokie. Schwartz could see him wavering. And, after the meeting, Smith told Schwartz that Skokie had to go into court to make sure the Nazis were kept out. Twenty years later Schwartz would comment, "You want to lead, you have to get out in front." He protested the order when Smith issued it but made the First Amendment argument to no avail. The mayor and village council directed Schwartz to get an injunction keeping the demonstration from taking place, and so on April 27 he filed papers in what became the case of *Skokie v. National Socialist Party of America.*

CHAPTER 2

The ACLU, the Supreme Court, and the First Amendment

One comment that often appears in letters I receive is that, if the Nazis come to power, the ACLU and its leaders would not be allowed to survive. Of course, that is true.

ARYEH NEIER, EXECUTIVE DIRECTOR, ACLU (1977)

Skokie corporation counsel Harvey Schwartz was born in 1929 and lived through World War II before being admitted to the bar in 1956. David Goldberger, the ACLU lawyer who would oppose Schwartz in court, was born in 1941, too late to remember much about the Second World War. Goldberger learned about the Holocaust, however, from his Jewish parents and from the rabbis at the synagogue the family attended. He also studied the American tradition of free speech as a law student at the University of Chicago. After passing the Illinois bar examination in 1968, he went to work as the legal director of the American Civil Liberties Union of Illinois. He left the ACLU in 1973 to work at the Legal Assistance Foundation, but returned to the Illinois affiliate in 1975. In 1977 he was its legal director.

The national American Civil Liberties Union (ACLU) was founded in 1920 in New York, in large part to protest government abridgment of the free speech of pacifists who opposed American involvement in World War I. Its genesis lay in the traditional American distrust of government and the belief that the rights of the people had to be kept safe from government encroachment. It was also in keeping with American tradition for the fledgling ACLU to concentrate on litigation.

Chief Justice John Marshall had proclaimed the existence of a strong independent judiciary in 1803, when his opinion for the Supreme Court in *Marbury v. Madison* stated that it was the duty of federal judges to negate any legislation that ran counter to the mandate of the Constitution. "It is emphatically the province and duty of the Judicial Department to say what the law is," he wrote. That encouraged an already litigious population to turn to the courts as well as to the legislatures when it felt the government was out of line with the will of the people as embodied in the Constitution. So while the founders of the ACLU did utilize appeals to the public, their major focus was on the courts, and that remained the case in 1977. The ACLU had become a presence by then in Washington and in many of the state capitals, with staff and volunteers lobbying legislators about bills that were pending or others that the ACLU thought should be written. It had developed a public-relations component in the belief that the best defense of civil liberties is an educated electorate. But the public knew the ACLU best as a litigating body, and it had become a magnet for attorneys, like David Goldberger, who wanted to devote themselves to the cause of civil liberties.

The ACLU had grown in substance as well as in numbers since 1920. No longer a handful of people on the East Coast, it was a nationwide organization with 200,000 members and branches in almost every state. It had extended its mandate to include all aspects of civil liberties and rights, working in areas such as religious freedom, the rights of the accused, and racial and gender equality. Its main task, however, still was protection of the speech clause of the First Amendment.

————

The First Amendment, part of the Bill of Rights that was added to the Constitution in 1791, reflected the suspicion many early Americans had of concentrated governmental power. As they read the draft constitution in 1787, with its plan for the establishment of a national government, they became afraid that the government created under it would be powerful enough to violate their rights. The Constitution's framers had assumed that since the proposed government was to have only those powers listed in the document, none of which seemed to suggest the authority to abridge rights, a specific reservation of such rights to the people and to the states was unnecessary. Delegates to a number of the state constitutional conventions organized to ratify the Constitution, however, declined to endorse it until they were assured that the first Congress would send the states suggested amendments spelling out the rights protected from abridgment by the federal government. The First Amendment therefore reads, "Congress shall make no law . . . abridging the freedom of speech, or of the press; or the right of the people peaceably to assemble, and to petition the Government for a redress of grievances."

The amendment was written as a limitation on Congress (and, through it, the entire federal government), and in effect left the states with a monopoly on violations of individual rights. Chief Justice John Marshall gave the formal imprimatur to the monopoly when he declared for the Supreme Court in 1833 *(Barron v. Baltimore)* that the Bill of Rights was binding only on the federal government, not the states. The states had their own and differing constitutions, and many were less protective of rights than was the federal Constitution. Whether or not they chose to be bound by similar restrictions was entirely up to them.

That remained the situation until 1925 and the case of *Gitlow v. New York.* Upholding the conviction of a Socialist for distributing a pamphlet that the New York government interpreted as advocating violent overthrow of the government, the Supreme Court declared that the First Amendment's speech and press clauses were binding on the states. The vehicle used by the Court for the holding was the Fourteenth Amendment's due process clause, which reads in part, "No State shall . . . deprive any person of life, liberty, or property, without due process of law." There is no indication in the amendment of exactly what the word "liberty" means. During the late nineteenth and early twentieth centuries, the Court had interpreted "liberty" as the right to acquire and control property. Justice Edward T. Sanford, speaking for the majority of the Court in *Gitlow,* began the process by which the amendment would be applied to civil liberties when he wrote, "for present purposes, we may and do assume that freedom of speech and of the press . . . are among the fundamental personal rights and 'liberties' protected by the due process clause of the Fourteenth Amendment from impairment by the States." The argument had been used by ACLU lawyer Walter H. Pollak, who wrote the Supreme Court brief in which Benjamin Gitlow appealed from his conviction in New York. An interesting side note is that Gitlow's trial lawyer, who had argued unsuccessfully that the pamphlet was a statement of abstract doctrine rather than an incitement to disorder, was the renowned Clarence Darrow.

———

The city of Chicago imposed its insurance requirement on Frank Collin and the NSPA in 1976. The Nazi who would deny Jews personhood as well as their right to speech promptly took his plight to the Illinois ACLU's Jewish legal director, asking him to defend the First Amendment rights of those who denied the right of others to speak. Goldberger and the ACLU had no hesitation about taking the case. For more than fifty years the ACLU's position had been that it was more dangerous to allow the government to pick and choose the speech it could forbid than to allow unpopular and even obnoxious speech to be spoken in public. Collin may not have been the ACLU's ideal American, but he had the same rights against illegitimate government power as anyone else. The Illinois ACLU had represented him for at least six years in his attempts to demonstrate in Chicago. So it was not surprising that Collin turned to Goldberger again when he learned on the afternoon of April 27, 1977, that Harvey Schwartz had filed papers to keep the NSPA from demonstrating in Skokie. Barbara O'Toole, the other ACLU lawyer in the case, would comment, "He [Collin] needed help; we needed to keep the law clean. It would not have served our interests to let him flounder without counsel and get injunctions against speech that would have been affirmed and then cited against us. It was very much in our interest to keep the law in order," by which she meant thoroughly grounded in the principles behind the First Amendment. The entire Illinois ACLU legal staff consisted of Goldberger, part-time volunteer O'Toole, and one other lawyer, all of whom were overloaded with cases. They didn't anticipate much difficulty with the Skokie case, however, so Goldberger and O'Toole went to court in the happily innocent belief that it would not take up too much of their time.

The papers Harvey Schwartz filed with the Circuit Court of Cook County, the county of which Skokie is a part, stated that approximately 40,500 of Skokie's 70,000 residents were Jewish. In recent days some of them had been frightened by ringing telephones between 3 and 5 A.M., the callers identifying themselves as Nazi Party members. Leaflets had been distributed in Skokie by the NSPA. Those acts, and the resultant media coverage, had alerted the Jewish community. Members of it were "taking measures unknown to the plaintiff to thwart the threatened march," creating a potentially violent situation. Schwartz referred to the leaflets, headed "Smash the Nazis," "No Free Speech for Fascists," and "Join Us [on] May Day," that were circulating in Skokie. The demonstration was a "deliberate and willful attempt to . . . incite racial and religious hatred" that presented a "grave and serious threat to the peace." Any display of the swastika in Skokie would be so severe a "symbolic assault" on the hundreds of Holocaust survivors and their families, as well as other Jewish residents, that it would constitute "incitation to violence and retaliation." For the sake of keeping the peace in Skokie, the demonstration had to be stopped.

The evening of April 27 was warm and springlike in Chicago. It was a nice time to spend with the family, and that is what David Goldberger was doing when Collin called him at home. Goldberger in turn called David Hamlin, the Illinois ACLU's executive director, and Edwin Rothschild, its president. Hamlin, thirty-four years old, was to become a major player in the Skokie situation. He had been with the ACLU since 1970, when he accepted the job of executive director of the New Hampshire ACLU. Before that, he had worked with community organizers under a federally funded program. He moved to Chicago and the directorship of the Illinois ACLU affiliate in 1974. Eventually he and Goldberger would share much of the responsibility for the Skokie situation, with Goldberger in charge of the legal side and Hamlin making some two hundred speeches about the case. Before one of those speeches, in a Skokie synagogue in June 1977, Hamlin got a telephone call from someone who warned, "You will not leave Skokie if you come." He promptly called the Skokie police, who turned out in force to protect him. Skokie was ready to safeguard the speech of someone whose message was almost as offensive to the survivors as Collin's—but then, he didn't bear the Nazi label.

Goldberger, Hamlin, and Rothschild felt, in Rothschild's words, "We have no choice but to take the case." In their judgment the village's action was an egregious one, and they knew that without the ACLU Collin would go unrepresented in the courts. The danger that concerned them was not that one Nazi's message would go unheard but that a dangerous precedent would be set for any municipality that disliked the speech of someone else. Chief Justice Warren Burger had recently written, in *Nebraska Press Association v. Stuart* (1976), that "prior restraints on speech and publication [stopping speech before it can be spoken or printed] are the most serious and the least tolerable infringement on First Amendment rights." Goldberger, Hamlin, and Rothschild were in complete agreement with that position. They also knew that they were getting the Illinois ACLU into what would be a controversial case and that time forced them to do so without first checking with the Illinois board of directors.

That was a problem for them because every ACLU state affiliate is the responsibility of a board of directors, made up of volunteers who are elected by ACLU members in their state. The executive director and staff do the day-to-day work, but the policies they carry out are mandated by the state board of directors and by a similar national board of directors. In mid-April 1977, the Illinois board discussed the affiliate's defense of Collin's right to march in Chicago. The staff decided to prepare the board for the litigation by showing it a police film of Collin's last Marquette Park demonstration in 1976. What the board saw was Collin, following exactly the same route his previous march had taken, being told by police that he had to turn his followers around and end the demonstration. The police were under orders, they said, to arrest him if he said "anything derogatory." He started to tell his marchers that the police were turning the march back and was promptly arrested. (He was later acquitted.)

The board, repelled by Collin and his ideas but equally aware of the free speech principle at stake, nonetheless found the issue of continued representation of him to be troublesome. A meeting for further discussion was scheduled for May 4. Now, before that discussion could take place, staff members Goldberger and Hamlin were proposing that they go ahead and represent Collin in Skokie. Edwin Rothschild decided to make the judgment his own responsibility and, speaking as the board's president, told Goldberger, "This is no problem; I'm ordering you to take the case." Rothschild was certain that the rest of the board would agree with his decision.

Goldberger then telephoned a number of attorneys who regularly volunteered their services for ACLU clients. All said they were too busy to prepare the case and be in court the next morning or that they declined to represent the NSPA. There was no alternative: the ACLU staff would have to represent Collin.

Goldberger next called Barbara O'Toole, a part-time staff lawyer. O'Toole, born in 1938, had gone to St. Mary's College at Notre Dame for her B.A. Returning to school some years later, she earned her law degree at Chicago's Loyola University, and she was admitted to the bar in 1969. She got a job working for the Illinois ACLU three days a week when another staffer went on maternity leave. The money for O'Toole's part-time position disappeared when the staffer returned, and O'Toole left the ACLU for a year. She then decided to work for the affiliate as a volunteer counsel, going into the office for two days a week, later extended to three. Her field of specialization was litigation on First Amendment issues in general, speech in particular.

Now she heard David Goldberger describing the Skokie situation and asking, "Are you up for this?" "Sure," she replied, and the two of them went to the ACLU office to plan strategy.

––––––

Goldberger and O'Toole didn't have to discuss the basis for their objection to the injunction. They knew they would rely on the First Amendment, as it had been interpreted by the United States Supreme Court since *Gitlow*.

While the *Gitlow* Court articulated the position that "liberty," at a minimum, included the rights to speech and press, it nonetheless upheld both Gitlow's conviction and the New York statute he was contesting. The Court first applied the *Gitlow* doctrine by striking down a state law in 1931, when it decided the case of *Stromberg v. California.* Nineteen-year-old Yetta Stromberg was convicted of displaying a red flag at a children's summer camp. The California legislature, noting that the red flag was used by Communist revolutionaries in what became the Soviet Union, had made its display in California a felony on the grounds that it was a symbol of opposition to the government and an invitation to public disorder. A seven-justice majority of the Court voted to overturn Stromberg's conviction, finding the law too vague and therefore a violation of the "liberty" protected by the Fourteenth Amendment. The decision enshrined the *Gitlow* doctrine in American law. To this day, the Fourteenth Amendment is assumed to make the First Amendment applicable to the states.

That assumption is responsible for an ironic twist of history—one, as we shall see, that makes speech jurisprudence in the United States quite different from that of other countries. Because the First Amendment was directed only at the federal government, it was written as an absolute: Congress was to make "no law" whatsoever limiting the right to speech. The states, however, routinely limited that right. Some limitations were relatively innocuous ones on "time, place, and manner." This meant, for example, that the states could prohibit loud public speeches in the middle of the night or political demonstrations on crowded city streets. Other abridgments of speech, such as the one at issue in *Stromberg,* were less benign and in effect enabled the government to take sides in a political debate by limiting speech it didn't like. Few people would question the societal utility of having the states promulgate time, place, and manner regulations. But once the words "no law" were held to limit *state* action, the burden of proof—that is, showing whether a state law was an unconstitutional violation of the right to speech—began to be shifted from the speaker to the state government.

This is an important point, and one that applies to all First Amendment/ Fourteenth Amendment jurisprudence. The speech clause was designed to apportion power between the federal government and the states, not to differentiate between societally useful speech and speech that might be repugnant to the public. A decision was made by the state constitutional conventions, the first Congress, and the states that ratified the First Amendment that it was undesirable to allow the *federal* government to make judgments about the legitimacy or illegitimacy of speech. That is why the word "no" is used in the phrase, "Congress shall make no law"—not "some" law or "only laws concerning time, place, and manner" or "only laws safeguarding national security." When *Gitlow* and *Stromberg* were handed down, however, there was no such societal debate. The Supreme Court interpreted the Constitution, as is its function, and that interpretation was accepted by the country. The question of whether it was appropriate and societally advantageous to prohibit *states* from regulating speech based on its content was never discussed by the electorate as a whole. The courts clearly were going to uphold statutes embodying time, place, and manner regulations. The implication was that they would interpret "no law" to mean "no law except those considered acceptable by the courts"—including time, place, and manner statutes. And that, in turn, set the stage for unceasing battles over whether the courts ought to permit additional limitations by the states on the right to speech.

One question involved in the battles was about the reason for the societal endorsement of the right to free speech. Supreme Court Justice Oliver Wendell Holmes Jr. implicitly referred to ideas found in John Milton's *Areopagitica* and John Stuart Mill's *On Liberty* when he wrote, in *Abrams v. United States* (1919),

> When men have realized that time has upset many fighting faiths, they may come to believe . . . that the best test of truth is the power of the thought to get itself accepted in the competition of the market, and that truth is the only ground upon which their wishes safely can be carried out.

Holmes thus saw the "marketplace of ideas" as one in which the clash of ideas would produce truth. The electorate would act as consumers, choosing those ideas that sounded right to them and rejecting others. Concurring in *Whitney v. California* (1927),*Justice Louis D. Brandeis articulated a related rationale, which is that free speech is particularly necessary in a democracy:

> Those who won our independence believed that the final end of the State was to make men free to develop their faculties, and that, in its

---

*Although Brandeis concurred because of a legal technicality, he disagreed with the reasoning of the majority, and so his opinion reads like a dissent.

government, the deliberative forces should prevail over the arbitrary. They valued liberty both as an end, and as a means. They believed liberty to be the secret of happiness, and courage to be the secret of liberty. They believed that freedom to think as you will and to speak as you think are means indispensable to the discovery and spread of political truth; that, without free speech and assembly, discussion would be futile; that, with them, discussion affords ordinarily adequate protection against the dissemination of noxious doctrine; that the greatest menace to freedom is an inert people; that public discussion is a political duty, and that this should be a fundamental principle of the American government.

"Free speech and assembly," Brandeis continued, are "functions essential to effective democracy." Democracy cannot exist without an educated electorate, he argued, and there could be no educated electorate in the absence of the freedom to hear and discuss all ideas. He spoke of both speech and assembly, as the First Amendment does, because citizens could be expected to assemble to hear and react to ideas. The same approach to speech as vital to a democratic polity can be found in Thomas Jefferson's statement that if he had to choose between a free government and a free press, he would opt for the latter. His choice reflected the knowledge that a democratic government cannot exist in the absence of electoral access to all ideas and that the press is a major conveyer of ideas. One might argue that the rights to free speech and press, therefore, are at least as much the rights to hear and read as they are to speak and write: all are necessary components of a democracy.

Holmes took the position that free speech had to be protected from government interference if truth was to be found; Brandeis, that it was essential in a democracy. Yet another argument for free speech is that it is necessary if individuals are to exploit their full potential and develop into complete and autonomous human beings. This was a second element of Brandeis's view, as seen in his statement that the "final end of the State" is "to make men free to develop their faculties" and that the founding generation had rightly "believed liberty to be the secret of happiness and courage to be the secret of liberty." A third rationale came from legal scholar Thomas I. Emerson, who wrote in 1970 that freedom of expression was "a method of achieving a more adaptable and hence a more stable community." Emerson believed that "people are more ready to accept decisions that go against them if they have a part in the decision-making process" and that freedom of expression "provides a framework in which the conflict necessary to the progress of a society can take place without destroying the society." Professor Norman Dorsen added in 1988 that free speech provides protection "against possible government corruption and excess" by permitting the exposure and questioning of governmental actions. He also suggested that in the United States, a redistribution of societal power would be impossible in the absence of speech rights for those who advocate such alteration of the status quo. Advocates presumably would include people of color, women, gay-rights activists, and so on.

All of these are arguments for keeping speech safe from the government. The First Amendment, as we have seen, was designed as a list of some of the rights with which the federal government could not interfere. But not only is the Constitution silent on the question of what rights might be abridged by state and local *governments,* it offers no guidance on the subject of whether *individual citizens* might have good reason to limit the speech of other citizens and to ask the government to help them in doing so.

For the survivors in Skokie, this was the crux of the issue. The ACLU saw itself as holding the line against the government as censor. The survivors and other critics of the ACLU's action viewed it as an endorsement of racist speech either on the grounds that hate speech was socially useful or on the grounds that it was relevant to policy discussions in a democracy. The ACLU was saying, "We don't want the *government* deciding what speech citizens can hear." The village of Skokie, however, was saying, "In permitting speech to be heard, the government is endorsing it. And some speech should not be uttered in a society where the government exists to protect the dignity of all." A view of the government as negative, as a potential violator of rights, clashed with that of a government as a guardian of the psychological as well as the physical well-being of its citizens. The clash would be repeated in the campus hate speech debates of the 1980s and 1990s.

Just a few years before it declared the rights of speech and press to be limitations on state governments, the Supreme Court found itself wrestling with the question of whether the First Amendment really meant that Congress could make "no law." The issue arose when Charles Schenck, secretary of a socialist party, was found guilty of "causing and attempting to cause insubordination in the military and naval forces of the United States, and to obstruct the recruiting and enlistment service of the United States" by sending new draftees a pamphlet describing the draft as unconstitutional. Congress and the president had criminalized such actions when they enacted the federal Espionage Act of June 15, 1917, in response to the outbreak of World War I. The authors of the First Amendment, of course, had not contemplated such a thing as national conscription and so had not addressed the issue of limitations upon criticism of it.

In 1919 and the case of *Schenck v. United States*, however, the Court was confronted with just such a situation. Justice Oliver Wendell Holmes Jr., writing for all nine justices, held that while under other circumstances the pamphlet might have been innocuous and within legal limits, "the character of every act depends upon the circumstances in which it is done." "When a nation is at war," he continued, "many things that might be said in time of peace are such a hindrance to its effort that their utterance will not be endured so long as men fight." The "circumstance" of war might criminalize speech that would be legal in peacetime. Turning to another possible "circumstance," Holmes offered what became a famous example of impermissible speech: "The most stringent protection of free speech would not protect a man in falsely shouting fire in a theatre and causing a panic." The criterion for illicit speech, according to Holmes, was "whether the words used are used in such circumstances and are of such a nature as to create a clear and present danger that they will bring about the substantive evils that Congress has a right to prevent."

The "clear and present danger" test would be invoked repeatedly by opponents of the Nazis' proposed demonstration in Skokie. Unfortunately, the test raised more questions than it answered. What was the meaning of "clear," and who was to decide whether a specific danger was "clear"? Did the danger have to be "clear" to all those people aware of the situation? If not, what proportion of them was sufficient to determine clarity? Similarly, what did "present" mean? Or, for that matter, "danger"? What were "the substantive evils that Congress has a right to prevent"? Did they include the possibility that young men might be persuaded that the draft was unconstitutional? The Court in effect said "yes" to that question when it upheld Schenck's conviction.

The ambiguity of the clear and present danger test was made strikingly clear only two years later, in *Abrams v. United States* (1919). There, a 7–2 majority of the Court upheld a conviction under the Sedition Act of 1918,

which made it a crime to "utter, print, write, or publish any disloyal, pro-
fane, scurrilous, or abusive language" about the United States' form of
government or to "urge, incite, or advocate any curtailment of production"
of things "necessary or essential to the prosecution of the war." Justice John
H. Clarke spoke for the Court in finding that two leaflets written and distributed by Abrams and his friends, which condemned President Woodrow
Wilson for sending American troops to fight in Soviet Russia and called
upon workers to strike in protest, constituted a clear and present danger
of interference with the war effort. The justice who dissented in the case
on behalf of himself and Justice Brandeis was Holmes. He argued that "the
surreptitious publishing of a silly leaflet by an unknown man" presented
no "clear and imminent danger."

If the justices could not agree on the meaning of clear, or present (now
altered by Holmes to "imminent"), or danger, how useful was the standard?
A similar situation arose in *Gitlow*, when Holmes, again writing for himself
and Brandeis, dissented from the Court's affirmation of Gitlow's conviction, declaring that speech separated from action could not be punished.
As to the question of danger, Holmes wrote, "The only difference between
the expression of an opinion and an incitement in the narrower sense is
the speaker's enthusiasm for the result." If the alleged danger was "incitement" to violent overthrow of the government, the totality of the circumstances had to be weighed. "Eloquence may set fire to reason," he
acknowledged, but he could not believe that the "redundant discourse" in
the pamphlets had any chance of starting "a present conflagration."

Holmes therefore saw no clear and present danger, while Justice Sanford
wrote for the majority of seven that such a danger existed. If, as Holmes
suggested, the difference between speech and incitement was the enthusiasm of the speaker, what legal rule could be employed to measure it? When
did speech cross an invisible line and become incitement, other than in the
obvious example of a speaker urging listeners to "follow me!" and participate in an illegal act "right now"?

Brandeis later regretted having gone along with the other justices in the
Schenck case and attempted to redefine the test in a series of opinions. "The
constitutional right of free speech has been declared to be the same in peace
and in war," he wrote in dissenting in another Espionage Act case (*Schaefer
v. United States*, 1920), thereby deliberately misreading what Holmes had
said in *Schenck*. Brandeis warned that it was precisely in time of war that
"an intolerant majority" was most likely to be "swayed by passion or by

fear," implying that freedom of speech was at least as necessary then as it was in peacetime. In dissent in yet a third Espionage Act case (*Pierce v. United States*, 1920), he reiterated his belief that speech had to be protected: "The fundamental right of free men to strive for better conditions through new legislation and new institutions will not be preserved, if efforts to secure it by argument to fellow citizens may be construed as criminal incitement to disobey the existing law." Holmes signed on to Brandeis's dissents in *Schaefer* and *Pierce*, indicating his agreement with this radical restatement of the clear and present danger test he had formulated.

The doctrine was refined again in *Whitney v. California*, which reached the Court in 1927. Anita Whitney was convicted by California of organizing, assisting in organizing, and being a member of a party, the Communist Labor Party, that advocated the use of unlawful force. The "organizational" effort in question was her attendance at a party convention. During it, she advocated a purely nonviolent role for the party. The convention nonetheless adopted a more violence-oriented platform, and she was charged and found guilty in spite of having expressed her continuing disagreement with it.

The majority of the Court voted to uphold the legitimacy of the statute and of Whitney's conviction. Brandeis thought the law was unconstitutional and explained in a concurrence the way he considered it to violate the clear and present danger test:

> To justify suppression of free speech there must be reasonable ground to fear that serious evil will result if free speech is practiced. There must be reasonable ground to believe that the danger apprehended is imminent. There must be reasonable ground to believe that the evil to be prevented is a serious one.

Even "advocacy of law-breaking" was "not a justification for denying free speech where the advocacy falls short of incitement and there is nothing to indicate that the advocacy would be immediately acted on." He reiterated his approach to the clear and present and danger test:

> In order to support a finding of clear and present danger it must be shown either that immediate serious violence was to be expected or was advocated, or that the past conduct furnished reason to believe that such advocacy was then contemplated. . . . [N]o danger flowing from speech can be deemed clear and present, unless the incidence of the evil apprehended is so imminent that it may befall before there is opportu-

nity for full discussion. If there be time to expose through discussion the falsehood and fallacies, to avert the evil by the processes of education, the remedy to be applied is more speech, not enforced silence.

Again, "imminent" was substituted for "present," and it was defined as triggering the evil before full discussion of what the speaker said was possible. This presumably differentiated legal advocacy from the "follow me right now" kind of situation. And Brandeis went even further. The only danger he would acknowledge as meeting the test was "the probability of serious injury to the State." Other violence or "destruction of property" could be punished if it was the immediate result of speech, but the speech itself had to be allowed.

The Court, as we will see in the next chapter, eventually adopted much of the Brandeis approach to speech.

CHAPTER 3

Why Free Speech Is Not Always Free

"Fighting" words—those which, by their very utterance,
inflict injury or tend to incite an immediate breach of the peace.

JUSTICE FRANK MURPHY,

Chaplinsky v. New Hampshire (1942)

Joseph Beauharnais might have been an earlier version of Frank Collin. He too was a resident of Illinois; he too spent his days vilifying a group of people because they were "different." The case he brought to the Supreme Court in 1952 would be invoked frequently in *Skokie* and was an obstacle that Goldberger and O'Toole had to confront.

Unlike Collin, Beauharnais did not choose both Jewish and African Americans as his targets; he confined himself to attacking the second. As president of the White Circle League of America, Beauharnais had his group distribute pamphlets on downtown Chicago street corners. The pamphlets included a petition calling upon the mayor and council of Chicago to enact segregation laws. They also urged "one million self respecting white people in Chicago to unite," and added, "If persuasion and the need to prevent the white race from becoming mongrelized by the Negro will not unite us, then the aggressions . . . rapes, robberies, knives, guns and marijuana of the Negro, surely will." Appended was an application for membership in the White Circle.

Beauharnais was charged in Chicago's municipal court and subsequently convicted of violating the 1917 Illinois statute that made it illegal to "present or exhibit in any public place . . . any lithograph . . . [which] portrays depravity, criminality, unchastity, or lack of virtue of a class of citizens, of any race, color, creed or religion . . . [and which] exposes the citizens of any race, color, creed or religion to contempt, derision, or obloquy." He appealed the conviction, and the case eventually reached the Supreme Court (*Beauharnais v. Illinois*, 1952). There, Justice Felix Frankfurter spoke for a five-justice majority, articulating what came to be known as the "group libel" doctrine. It, along with the doctrines of preferred freedoms and prior restraint, would become as important to the *Skokie* case as the doctrine of fighting words.

.

The American colonists brought the complementary concepts of criminal and civil libel with them from England. Criminal libel can be prosecuted by the government; civil libel can be the basis of a lawsuit brought by an individual. The colonists and later Americans defined libel as malicious public defamation of a person, tending to "expose one to public hatred, shame, obloquy, contumely, odium, contempt, ridicule, aversion, ostracism, degradation, or disgrace, or to induce an evil opinion of one in the minds of right-thinking persons, and to deprive one of their confidence and friendly intercourse in society." The assumption was that a libel damaged one's reputation, and the burden of proof was placed on the alleged libeler to demonstrate a legal justification for his or her words. Initially, truth was not a defense, although courts gradually turned it into one in the decades after the Constitution was adopted. They also held that malicious use of even "fair comment," meaning opinions about matters of general interest, was actionable. As the Supreme Court stated in *Cantwell v. Connecticut* (1940), "resort to epithets or personal abuse is not in any proper sense communication of information or opinion safeguarded by the Constitution." The Court's approach in *Cantwell* was validated in *Chaplinsky v. New Hampshire* (1942), discussed below.

Some nineteenth-century judges were concerned that the doctrines of civil and criminal libel could limit the free flow of speech necessary to a democracy as well as the citizenry's information about possible malfeasance by public officials and candidates. They created a permissible area in which commentators on the public conduct of officials and candidates could write or speak, as long as their criticism was meant to inform and was not malicious.

The law of libel usually was applied to individuals, not to groups, and Justice Hugo Black would point that out in his dissenting opinion in *Beauharnais*. Frankfurter attempted to answer Black's assertion by writing, "[I]f an utterance directed at an individual may be the object of criminal sanctions, we cannot deny to a state power to punish the same utterance directed at a defined group." A group was in effect viewed as simply as a collection of individuals, and Frankfurter considered Illinois's experience with violence directed at racial groups to be relevant in assessing the constitutionality of the statute. If "willful purveyors of falsehood concerning racial and religious groups" were part of Illinois history and Illinois concluded that they obstructed the "free, ordered life in a metropolitan, polyglot community," then the state had the power to outlaw their public utterances. Frankfurter cited the racial violence that was a factor in Illinois public life at least as early as the murder of abolitionist Elijah Lovejoy in 1837 and as recently as the racial rioting that took place in East St. Louis four days after the law was enacted. "We would deny experience," he said, "to say that the Illinois legislature was without reason in seeking ways to curb false or malicious defamation of racial and religious groups, made in public places and by means calculated to have a powerful emotional impact on those to whom it was presented."

Frankfurter clearly disliked the law. He emphasized that the decision reflected appropriate judicial deference to state legislatures rather than approval of the statute. He noted that "the legislative remedy might not in practice mitigate the evil, or might itself raise new problems" and that "our finding that the law is not constitutionally objectionable carries no implication of approval of the wisdom of the legislation or of its efficacy." Misguided as the law might be, Frankfurter said, enactment of it was clearly within the legislature's power.

Justice Black disagreed about the validity of the law. To him, there was no doubt that however offensive their opinions, Beauharnais and the White Circle were "making a genuine effort to petition their elected representatives," a right sanctioned by the First Amendment. Criminal libel, as he understood it, was the offense of defaming an *individual*, and he disagreed that libel law could be expanded to apply to groups. "Every expansion of the law of criminal libel so as to punish discussions of matters of public concern means a corresponding invasion of the area dedicated to free expression by the First Amendment," he warned. "Ironically enough," he added, "the same kind of state law that makes Beauharnais a criminal for advocating segregation in Illinois can be utilized to send people to jail in other states for advocating equality and nonsegregation." Black thus forecast the assertion that would be made in *Skokie* that if Nazi speech could be forbidden in Illinois, the same standard, speech offensive to the community, could have been used by a southern state to outlaw protests by civil rights activists in the 1950s and 1960s.

Justice Stanley Reed, also dissenting, questioned the specificity of the words "virtue," "derision," and "obloquy" in the statute. They were so vague, he argued, that the law could not fulfill its purposes of letting speakers know what was permissible and telling the courts which speech could be punished. The Court had already held overly vague speech-limiting statutes to be unconstitutional.

Justice William O. Douglas took another tack, similar to the one Brandeis had followed in *Whitney.* Acknowledging that "Hitler and his Nazis showed how evil a conspiracy could be which was aimed at destroying a race by exposing it to contempt, derision, and obloquy," Douglas nonetheless read the First Amendment as forbidding limitations on speech unless "the peril of speech [is] clear and present, leaving no room for argument, raising no doubts as to the necessity of curbing speech in order to prevent disaster." He echoed Black in writing that while upholding Beauharnais's conviction affected a white man, under the same reasoning, "tomorrow a Negro will be haled before a court for denouncing lynch law in heated terms." "Farm laborers in the West who compete with field hands drifting up from Mexico" and "a minority which finds employment going to members of the dominant religious group" would be equally affected. The decision gave state governments "the power to control unpopular blocs." It was "a warning to every minority that when the Constitution guarantees free speech it does not mean what it says."

Justice Black added that "no legislature is charged with the duty or vested with the power to decide what public issues Americans can discuss." Although he did not mention *Gitlow,* he cited subsequent decisions to the effect that the words "make no law" in the First Amendment were made equally applicable to the states. "Make no law" meant precisely that, Black thundered, and added, "I reject the holding that either state or nation can punish people for having their say in matters of public concern."

Black took what has been called the "absolutist" position, insisting that "no law" permitted no regulation whatsoever of any speech. He was alone in sustaining that position almost throughout his long tenure on the Court. The Court has held instead that speech with no social value, as the Court majority has labeled pornography and libel of private individuals, can be prohibited.

The Court has nonetheless declined to apply the *Beauharnais* doctrine to other cases, apparently having decided on second thought that the group libel approach it used there is not a tenable one. If negative public statements about groups are impermissible, the justices may have reasoned, discussions such as those about the validity or lack thereof of religious doctrine would be outlawed, as would claims by one religious or racial group that it had been discriminated against by another group. African Americans would not be able to speak in public about racism; Native Americans could not refer to their suffering at the hands of white Americans; West Coast Japanese Americans would not have been permitted to demand reparations for the period during World War II when they were summarily herded into relocation camps.

This seems to have been the thinking behind the Supreme Court's 1969 per curiam decision in *Brandenburg v. Ohio*. (A per curiam opinion is one handed down by the entire Court and not prefaced with the name of a specific justice.) Brandenburg, the leader of a Ku Klux Klan group, had invited a reporter at a Cincinnati television station to attend a Ku Klux Klan rally. With permission from the organizers, the reporter and a cameraman later broadcast portions of the films they took there. The film showed twelve figures in hooded Klan regalia, some of them carrying firearms, burning a large wooden cross. As the Supreme Court would note, most of the sound track was incomprehensible, but scattered phrases uttered by Brandenburg could be understood. He said in part,

> We're not a revengent organization, but if our President, our Congress, our Supreme Court, continues to suppress the white, Caucasian race, it's possible that there might have to be some revengeance taken....
>
> We are marching on Congress July the Fourth, four hundred thousand strong. From there, we are dividing into two groups, one group to march on St. Augustine, Florida, the other group to march into Mississippi.

A second speaker commented, "Personally, I believe the nigger should be returned to Africa, the Jew returned to Israel." Among other portions of the speeches that could be heard were the following:

> This is what we are going to do to the niggers.
> ... a dirty nigger ...
> Send the Jews back to Israel.
> Let's give them back to the dark garden.
> Save America.
> Let's go back to constitutional betterment.

Bury the niggers.
We intend to do our part.
Freedom for the whites.
... nigger will have to fight for every inch he gets from now on.

Brandenburg was convicted under a Ohio statute that criminalized "advocat[ing] ... the duty, necessity, or propriety of crime, sabotage, violence, or unlawful methods of terrorism as a means of accomplishing industrial or political reform."

The unsigned opinion for the Court noted that the decision in *Whitney*, upholding a similar conviction for syndicalism, had been "thoroughly discredited by later decisions." It endorsed the concurring opinion Justice Brandeis had written in that case and said of the Ohio statute,

> we are here confronted with a statute which, by its own words and as applied, purports to punish mere advocacy and to forbid, on pain of criminal punishment, assembly with others merely to advocate the described type of action. Such a statute falls within the condemnation of the First and Fourteenth Amendments.

The Court substituted the standard of "incitement to imminent lawless action" for "clear and present danger" and struck down the statute, seemingly negating the doctrine of group libel. In 1964, the Court had responded to a civil libel suit by deciding that even statements about public officials that turned out to be false were legal as long as they were not made in "reckless disregard" of the truth *(New York Times v. Sullivan)*. Justice Douglas was prescient when he wrote in *Beauharnais* that the next group libel case might involve a black American protesting lynch laws. In *Times v. Sullivan*, the plaintiff was a segregationist Montgomery, Alabama, police official. The defendants were four black ministers, leaders of the civil rights movement, who had placed a newspaper advertisement critical of his handling of civil rights demonstrations. Justice William Brennan wrote for a unanimous court that "freedom of expression upon public questions is secured by the First Amendment" and that the "profound national commitment to the principle that debate on public issues should be uninhibited, robust, and wide-open" was made in the knowledge that "erroneous statement is inevitable in free debate." The Court went on in *Rosenbloom v. Metromedia, Inc.* (1971) to give First Amendment protection to defamatory falsehoods about anyone, public official or not, when they occurred in a discussion of matters of public interest. That completed the demise, in practice if not in theory, of the group libel doctrine. Because the Court did not specifically overturn the doctrine, however, it could be referred to as a precedent by the town of Skokie.

One of its earlier doctrines that the Court *has* continued to utilize is that of "preferred freedoms." Writing for the Court in *U.S. v. Carolene Products* (1938), Justice Harlan Stone added a famous footnote to his declaration that the Court must assume statutes to be constitutional until proven otherwise. Reversing the burden of proof and putting it upon the government's shoulders in some cases, Stone wrote for the Court that the presumption of constitutionality might not apply "when legislation appears on its face to be within a specific prohibition of the Constitution, such as those of the first ten amendments, which are deemed equally specific when held to be embraced within the Fourteenth." Stone referred to "legislation which restricts those political processes which can ordinarily be expected to bring about repeal of undesirable legislation," meaning speech. The implication of his footnote is that most limitations on speech and on small unpopular groups are assumed to be invalid. The Court first applied the footnote in 1943 when it struck down a state statute used to prosecute Jehovah's Witnesses who distributed religious tracts *(Murdock v. Pennsylvania)*. Those arguing that some kinds of speech can be abridged must prove that limitations on them are within their power, and the Court usually has been skeptical of such claims.

Four years after the Court heard the *Carolene* case it rendered a verdict in *Chaplinsky v. New Hampshire* (1942). The question was whether an insult directed at a specific person in a public place was illegal. The literature that Chaplinsky, a Jehovah's Witness, was distributing on the streets of Rochester, New Hampshire, was described by passersby as a denunciation of all religion. Some of them immediately complained to the nearby city marshal, who replied that Chaplinsky was lawfully engaged, but who also warned Chaplinsky that the gathering crowd was getting restless. The marshal then left the scene for other duties. When violence erupted soon afterwards, a police officer took Chaplinsky in hand and started off for the local police station. On their way they encountered the city marshal, who repeated his warning, upon which Chaplinsky reportedly called him "a damned Fascist" and "a God damned racketeer." Chaplinsky was convicted under a state law that made it illegal to "address any offensive, derisive or annoying word to any other person who is lawfully in any street or other public place, [or] call him by any offensive or derisive name, [or] make any noise or exclamation in his presence and hearing with intent to deride, offend or annoy him, or to prevent him from pursuing his lawful business or occupation."

Upholding the law and the conviction, Justice Frank Murphy identified the kinds of speech that the Court believed were unprotected by the First Amendment:

> These include the lewd and obscene, the profane, the libelous, and the insulting or "fighting" words—those which, by their very utterance, inflict injury or tend to incite an immediate breach of the peace. It has been well observed that such utterances are no essential part of any exposition of ideas, and are of such slight social value as a step to truth that any benefit that may be derived from them is clearly outweighed by the social interest in order and morality.

If speech included "words likely to cause an average addressee to fight," it constituted incitement to violent breach of the peace.

The test relied on the "utilitarian" approach to speech; that is, if speech is unrelated to a search for truth, it can be prohibited. The concept of "'fighting' words—those which, by their very utterance, inflict injury or tend to incite an immediate breach of the peace"—was to loom large in the *Skokie* case. A speaker could be punished if his or her speech provoked *listeners* to breach the peace—not only if he or she meant to engage in violence—or inflicted injury upon them.

The Chaplinsky case established what scholar Harry Kalven would label the "heckler's veto": the power of listeners to stop speech because it is sufficiently disturbing to evoke a violent response or, in some undefined way, to harm them. This suggests another problem. While it will be explored further in chapter 8, some mention of it should be made here.

A major and perhaps primary reason for the establishment of governmental systems is to keep people and their property safe from violence. Violence, however, can be done by words as well as acts, as anyone who has been seriously offended by insults can attest. If we assume that words can wound, we must ask what constitutes a wound so harmful that it overcomes the societal interest in free speech. The speech of people who disagree with us can be wounding, even if politely worded, for it is a statement that our beliefs are wrong. Speech that is impolitely worded may be even more wounding. While Holmes said in *Abrams* that the effect of speech will vary according to the enthusiasm of the speaker, he might have added that it will also differ according to the words used. If a segregationist talks about "sending African Americans back to Africa," the speech may well hurt an African American who happens to hear it. If the thought is the same but the language is "send the niggers back where they belong," the speech will be even more offensive. If the speaker says, turning to a group of African Americans in the audience, "You niggers belong back in Africa, where you came from," the speech clearly has reached yet another level of offensiveness and, perhaps, of harm.

Can people claim the right to government protection from that kind of harm? Is psychological injury something that the state should prohibit? If so, how is it to be measured? If one person called "nigger" or "kike" or "bitch" or "pig" laughs it off but another does not, can the listener's reaction become cause for government action? Again: if so, at what point? It may cause me discomfort to listen to a statement I consider offensive. Is my discomfort, unshared by others, sufficient to render the speech illegal? What if two of us share the discomfort? three of us? ten? Does freedom of communication lose its function if only those ideas acceptable to all can be heard?

Equally, does speech fulfill its societal function if it is deliberately used to hurt? If so, how do we answer the question of who will be hurt by what? How will we measure whether hurt is caused "deliberately" rather than in the course of discussing an idea? What if someone speaks hurtful words deliberately but claims they were the only way to make a point? An example might be the argument, made in 1997 by a commission studying the armed forces, that they would be most efficient if they trained women separately from men. The announcement may well have hurt women listeners aware of the history of gender segregation policies in the United States as carrying implications of inferiority, but it came in the context of a valid discussion of ideas. If the criterion for banning speech is that it may cause psychological damage as well as social and economic harm, why does intent, rather than the extent of the harm, make a difference?

There is, in addition, the problem of how we differentiate among disagreement, discomfort, and real psychological harm. The conundrum would be at the heart of a separate case brought by Sol Goldstein and, eventually, of the plea made by the village of Skokie in various tribunals.

Skokie also involved the concept of prior restraint, which applies to a restriction put upon an act before it takes place. In speech jurisprudence, this means that a speaker is denied the right to speak or that a proposed publication is enjoined before it sees the light of day, rather than the speaker or publisher being allowed to proceed but being punished after the fact. Goldberger and O'Toole would argue in *Skokie* that prior restraint of speech was forbidden by the American constitution.

The Court declared prior restraint unconstitutional in 1931 *(Near v. Minnesota)*. Acting under a law that permitted suspension of periodicals that were "malicious, scandalous and defamatory," the state of Minnesota had enjoined further publication of the *Saturday Press*. The Minneapolis weekly newspaper was infamous for being virulently anti-Semitic, anti-Catholic, and anti-black. The state decided to close it down when one of its editions carried an article accusing specific public officials of participating in a gambling ring. The publishers appealed to the Supreme Court. Writing for a majority of five, Chief Justice Charles Evans Hughes declared that freedom of the press was part of the "liberty" guaranteed by the Fourteenth Amendment's due process clause and that if the First Amendment had any meaning it all, it was that almost all prior restraints were forbidden.

The prior restraint doctrine was also prominent in the case of *Rockwell v. Morris* (1960), brought in New York by neo-Nazi George Lincoln Rockwell—the same Rockwell who later threatened to demonstrate in Skokie on the Jewish High Holy Days. Rockwell sued after being denied a permit to use a New York City park for one of his demonstrations. The New York trial court said,

> A community need not wait to be subverted by street riots and storm troopers; but, also, it cannot, by its policemen or commissioners, suppress a speaker, in prior restraint, on the basis of news reports, hysteria, or inference that what he did yesterday, he will do today. Thus, too, if the speaker incites others to immediate unlawful action he may be punished—in a proper case, stopped when disorder actually impends;

but this is not to be confused with unlawful action from others who seek unlawfully to suppress or punish the speaker.

Unpopularity of views, the court continued, "is not enough. Otherwise, the preacher of any strange doctrine could be stopped; the anti-racist himself could be suppressed, if he undertakes to speak in 'restricted' areas; and one who asks that public schools be open indiscriminately to all ethnic groups could be lawfully suppressed, if only he chose to speak where persuasion is needed most." The Supreme Court refused to review the court's decision or the similar decision of the appellate court.

The leading prior-restraint case, *New York Times v. United States* (1971), was decided by the Court only six years before *Skokie*. The federal government attempted to stop the *Times* from publishing a classified Defense Department report on the history of American involvement in the Vietnam War, claiming publication constituted a threat to national security. Even in the face of that strong an assertion, the Supreme Court held that there could be no prior restraint because the government had not met the heavy burden of proof that might have permitted it. A majority of the justices would have made the evidentiary test an extremely stringent one, passable only if the government proved that disclosure of the information "surely" would result in "direct, immediate, and irreparable damage" to national security.

Stopping the NSPA's demonstration from ever taking place, as Skokie had asked the Illinois Circuit Court located in Chicago to do, therefore clearly ran counter to what had become the Supreme Court's and most lower courts' refusal to validate prior restraints. Skokie would argue that the restraint was nonetheless warranted in this case; the ACLU would argue as strenuously that it was not.

One final doctrine must be introduced if the legal complexities of the *Skokie* case are to be understood. It involves symbolic speech.

The Supreme Court has held that "speech" can mean the communication of ideas without anyone actually speaking. Such, for example, was the import of its holding in *Thornhill v. Alabama* (1940), when it declared picketing in support of a labor dispute to come under the protection of the First Amendment. For those without means to advertise their position through the mails or the mass media, peaceful picketing—silent or noisy—may be

{ *When the Nazis Came to Skokie* }

the only means of communication with the public that is available. (The demonstration the NSPA wanted to hold in Skokie was the legal equivalent of picketing.) It will be remembered that the Court had upheld Yetta Stromberg's right to display a red flag on the grounds of free speech. Similarly, the Court decided in 1969 that three students in Iowa junior high and senior high schools could not be suspended from school for wearing black armbands symbolizing their opposition to American involvement in the Vietnam War *(Tinker v. Des Moines)*. The armbands had no writing on them; the Court decided they constituted symbolic speech. In a decision one year earlier, however, the Court had validated a federal law that prohibited the mutilation of draft registration cards (*United States v. O'Brien,* 1968) on the theory that the law was meant to protect the government's interest in administering the draft rather than to stifle expression of a point of view. The Court thus has accepted the doctrine of symbolic speech but has taken various stands on its specific application.

The last speech case directly relevant to *Skokie* was *Cohen v. California,* another case arising during the Vietnam era that was decided by the Court in 1971. It concerned the jacket worn by Paul Robert Cohen in the corridor of a Los Angeles municipal courtroom.

Cohen, an antiwar protester, was in the courthouse on unrelated business when he was arrested because his jacket displayed the words "Fuck the Draft." He was convicted for disturbing the peace through "offensive conduct." As Justice John Marshall Harlan said in the opinion he wrote for himself and four other justices, "This case may seem at first blush too inconsequential to find its way into our books, but the issue it presents is of no small constitutional significance." It was whether the government had the power, "consonant with the Constitution, to shut off discourse solely to protect others from hearing it."

Harlan found no obscenity involved because there was nothing erotic about the message. Similarly, it could be not classified as fighting words because it was not directed at the person of the hearer. (Harlan implicitly indicated for the Court that fighting words meant one-on-one communication.) There was no captive audience because, Harlan wrote, "those in the Los Angeles courtroom could effectively avoid further bombardment of their sensibilities simply by averting their eyes." The issue of whether members of an audience could be placated by an admonition to avert their eyes would arise in Skokie, when the argument was made that those who found Nazi uniforms and swastikas upsetting could stay away from the proposed NSPA demonstration. If, as Harlan suggested, "averting their eyes" is the Constitution's directive to those who would find specific written expression in a public place offensive, then presumably staying away or putting one's hands over one's ears is the constitutional response to offensive spoken communications.

The appellate court of California had referred to "women and children" present in the courthouse as constituting grounds for punishing the written "speech," apparently thinking it was not sufficient to counsel them to look elsewhere. In the absence of obscenity, fighting words, or a captive audience, Harlan stated, the government's power to silence speech was "dependent upon a showing that substantial privacy interests are being invaded in an essentially intolerable manner" because a "broader view of their authority would effectively empower a majority to silence dissidents simply as a matter of personal predilections." Invasion of the privacy of people at home by a loudspeaker in the middle of the night, for example, could be banned. While Harlan recognized that people in a courthouse were not necessarily as free to leave as were those, for instance, in a public park, he held that what privacy invasion there might be in someone's apparel was too insubstantial to permit government regulation.

Why is a knowledge of these doctrines necessary if one is to understand the conflict in Skokie? Why was a dispute involving competing *values*—the value of speech, the value of being safeguarded from psychological harm—treated as one of possibly competing *laws,* with the First Amendment on the one hand and the Skokie ordinances on the other? Why was it necessary to invoke past Supreme Court decisions in order to decide what was right—not "legal" or "illegal," but *right?* The answer lies in part in the American attitude toward law and rights: our attitude to the judiciary in general and the Supreme Court in particular.

No other nation empowers its highest court to exercise the kind of policy-making power enjoyed by the United States Supreme Court—and, by extension, lower federal courts. Although judges usually define their function as "interpreting" law rather than making it, the Court's power to declare federal and state laws and actions constitutional or unconstitutional necessarily implies a policy-making role. When the Court holds that the Constitution prohibits prior restraints on speech, for example, it is helping to set the country's policy toward speech. When it decides that statutes limiting picketing by labor unions are unconstitutional, it is making policy about both speech and the status of unions. Similarly, the Court's decision in *Brown v. Board of Education* (1964), declaring segregated public school education to be in violation of the Fourteenth Amendment, began a major change in American policy toward African Americans and other people of color.

As Thomas Emerson noted in *A General Theory of the First Amendment,*

[I]n the United States today we have come to depend upon legal institutions and legal doctrines as a major technique for maintaining our system of free expression. We have developed and refined this technique more than has any other country. These legal institutions and ideas in turn affect public attitudes and philosophies; both philosophers and protest movements argue in terms of constitutional rights.

Had he been discussing other areas of law as well as speech, Emerson might have added that the United States, more than any other country, has delegated the definition of our rights in general to constitutional mandates and judicial interpretation.

It has been axiomatic in American political thought since the writing of the Declaration of Independence that governments are the creation of human beings who have inalienable rights. Those rights cannot be properly safeguarded in the absence of law, and the protection of rights is the major reason for the establishment of governments. Once a government is established, however, the question becomes, who will watch the watchdog? Won't a government sufficiently powerful to protect the individual's rights to life, liberty, and property from abridgment by others be at least as capable of violating those rights itself? If democracy implies rule by the majority, and the government is elected by the majority, might it not act as the majority wishes and ignore the rights of the unpopular?

The Founders answered these questions by emphasizing that democracy is not merely rule by the majority but, as important, formal protection of the rights of individuals. An independent judiciary is a necessary part of a democratic polity, for it alone can defend rights and liberties if the government attempts to violate them. The judiciary is the guardian of the Constitution—the basic law in which the people freely grant the government powers. The government is granted only some powers, not all the powers the government may seek. Among the powers the people retain for themselves is the power to decide, in periodic elections, whether officeholders should step aside in favor of others. The people have chosen not to give public officeholders the power to abridge individual liberties such as religion, speech and press, assembly, and so on. As a hedge against possible governmental misuse of power they create not only a judiciary but one that is truly independent of other branches of the government: a judiciary that, in the absence of malfeasance, holds its job for life and therefore does not have to pander to the whims of the Congress or president or whatever majority is temporarily in power.

As we have seen, the Court began stepping into a role as the guardian of free speech for the country in 1925, when it declared that the due process clause of the Fourteenth Amendment made the right to speech a limitation on state as well as federal power. The reliance of the American people on the Supreme Court was cemented in the 1950s and 1960s when, under Chief Justice Earl Warren, the Court acquired a reputation as both a protector of rights and a redefiner of them for a changing society. Americans frequently say "I got my rights," and they expect the courts to validate and protect those rights.

So Americans claim both unconditional possession of rights and a corollary right to have courts protect them. Rights, however, are not unconditional. Your "right" to swing your arm ends where my nose begins. Rights can be exercised only if they do not interfere with the rights of others. Sometimes rights conflict. Full exercise of the right to a free press, for example, may endanger an accused's chance of receiving a fair trial. Equally, taking all steps to ensure a fair trial may impede the right to a free press.

Skokie can be viewed as such a conflict of rights: the right of Frank Collin to speak and the asserted right of Sol Goldstein to be spared psychological trauma. When rights conflict, Americans turn to the courts for a resolution. What was a clash of values becomes a matter of constitutional interpretation. The question is transformed. It is no longer one about the positives and negatives of permitting public expression of "words that wound"; instead, it has become a query about whether or not certain acts fall within constitutional guidelines.

The benefit of giving such dilemmas to the courts to decide, Justice William J. Brennan believed, was that "judicial review has proved . . . to be vital and indispensable for the protection of the individual's liberty in our democratic society." He thought that only an independent judiciary would have the courage to uphold individual rights in a democratic state, where the government was elected by the majority. Unperturbed by the seeming twists and turns the courts had given to the doctrine of speech, Brennan wrote in 1988,

> We must keep in mind that while the words of the Constitution and the Bill of Rights are binding, their application to specific problems is not often easy.... Thus it is that the Constitution does not take the form of a litany of specifics....
>
> Where one man claims a right to speak and the other man claims the right to be protected from abusive or dangerously provocative remarks, the conflict [between individual and governmental power] is inescapable.

But, as Thomas Emerson commented, in spite of all the tests and doctrines the Court has fashioned in the area of speech, it "has never developed any comprehensive theory of what that constitutional guarantee means and how it should be applied in concrete cases." Whether public policy toward speech *should* depend on interpretation of a legal document rather than on a consideration of what is best for society is yet another question—one that was asked, in a way, by the citizens of Skokie.

CHAPTER 4

Judges, Lawyers, and Legislatures

*Lying opinions, than which no mental plague is greater, and vices which
corrupt the heart and moral life, should be diligently repressed by public authority,
lest they insidiously work the ruin of the state.*

POPE LEO XIII, *Libertas praestantissimum* (1888)

Judge Joseph Wosik arrived at Chicago's Richard J. Daley Civic Center on Thursday, April 28, ready to hear the case of *Skokie v. NSPA.* A Polish American born in 1913, Wosik was educated at DePaul University in Chicago and admitted to the Illinois bar in 1939, two years before the United States entered the Second World War. His career was interrupted when, like so many other young men, he was drafted. Wosik served with the army in Europe and returned to practice law in Chicago. In April 1977 he held the elected position of judge of the Circuit Court of Cook County.

Harvey Schwartz presented Skokie's case for an injunction that morning, quickly summarizing the argument he had made in the papers filed the previous day. "We will bring to this Court by way of the testimony of witnesses the present mood that prevails in the Village of Skokie," he said, "one that has been inflamed and incited only and simply by reason of the prospective *march* [emphasis added] by the defendants . . . which if it is not enjoined by this Court could lead to great violence and to irreparable harm." Then he called his five witnesses.

The first was Fred Richter, of the Synagogue Council, who said that he expected 12,000 to 15,000 people at the planned counterdemonstration. Asked to recall the April 21 meeting of the council and other groups, he testified,

> The speakers that spoke, I'll start with the survivors, spoke in strong, definitive terms that they cannot under any circumstances take the fact that a Nazi will walk on the streets of Skokie, that this is an outrage and an obscenity to them, that the very thought of seeing their uniforms in Skokie has gotten them beyond their rationality, and these are people who are in positions within business, leadership, very, very responsible

people who have lived here for many, many years and act within civic and within the other areas of life in the United States today.

Schwartz asked Richter about the mood of the people in Skokie:
Q: Is it anger?
A: It is rage, sir . . . it is not anger. It is rage.
Sol Goldstein followed Richter to the stand. He told the court that the swastika "reminds me [of] my closest family who were sent to death by the swastika, and it reminds me [of] a threat that I am not safe with my life. It reminds me that my children are not safe with their lives." The uniform worn by the NSPA, he said, "is the same uniform that sent people to gas chambers, to extermination camps." He did not *intend* to react violently to the sight of swastikas if the Nazi demonstration took place, but he was not certain he would be able to control himself and could not promise to refrain from attacking Collin. He assumed this reaction was shared by other Skokie residents, judging from the 1,100 people who had attended a protest meeting the previous Sunday. Over Goldberger's objection, he, too, was asked to describe the mood of people with whom he had spoken.

Q: And what is your opinion as to the mood?
A: It's large groups of people that won't allow it to overpower that this demonstration will take place. It will be a bloodshed. . . . It will be victims, it will be bloodshed, it will be damage of Village property. I don't know what it will be. It will be loss of lives, maybe.

These are people that lost their parents, their children, their wives, that know what it means a swastika to them. They promise to death that a swastika won't appear any more. They promised their children that came here . . . a peaceful life, and they cannot do it for the sake of their children that they will ever be threatened with a swastika, that means to them gas chambers at Auschwitz.

Schwartz went on to ask Goldstein about his attitude toward the proposed "march of the Nazis in Skokie." Goldstein replied,

This means to me two things. Number one, [the Nazis are saying] that two million survivors got . . . left alive, and to remind them that we are not through with you.

Number two is the heart of the Jewish population, to show them that the Nazi threat is not over, it can happen again.

Gilbert Gordon, the assistant village attorney, then took over from Schwartz. The first thing he did, again over Goldberger's objections, was call Frank Collin to the stand as an adverse witness.

Collin proudly admitted to the court that his group was responsible for a circular saying that Jews were behind the "black invasion of Southwest Chicago" and therefore would be targets of the NSPA's street demonstrations and speeches in the future. He told Wosik that while the demonstrators in Skokie would carry signs saying "Free Speech for Whites" and similar slogans, none would be anti-Semitic. He and his followers would make no speeches, nor would they distribute any literature.

Collin was followed to the stand by Mayor Albert Smith. Asked what he had counseled Skokie's rabbis to tell their congregations about the proposed demonstration, Smith replied, "To try and contain themselves . . . to ask their congregations to pray for these poor, misguided souls." Collin's reaction to Smith's words can be inferred from Judge Wosik's angry comment, "That isn't funny, Mr. Collin." Smith added that his conversations with community leaders and religious groups in Skokie had convinced him that uncontrollable violence would accompany any NSPA demonstration in Skokie.

Ronald Lanski, a Skokie resident and Skokie's final witness, talked about the "Smash the Nazis" leaflet he had seen, suggesting that feelings were running so high that violence was inevitable. With that, Skokie rested its case. There was no testimony from any Skokie police officer about what preparations for violence might be taken or about the police force's ability or lack of ability to handle the situation. Skokie did not argue that the Nazis' conduct would be criminal, but rather that residents of the village might be impelled to react violently.

Goldberger's opening remarks echoed the memorandum he and O'Toole had prepared, calling the request for an injunction a "classic case" of the government asking a court "to impose a prior restraint on the speech of persons advocating unpopular ideas." The burden of controlling potential violence should be placed on the shoulders of Skokie law enforcement officials, he argued, not on those of Collin and his followers. He also entered into evidence an affidavit in which Collin reiterated that his plan was for a short and orderly demonstration in front of the village hall.

Goldberger's argument did not persuade Judge Wosik, which came as no surprise to anyone in the courtroom. Soon after Schwartz began presenting his case, Judge Wosik's secretary interrupted and the judge left the bench briefly. He had a phone call from Cook County sheriff Richard Elrod, a figure in Chicago's Democratic machine. There was no doubt in the minds of the ACLU figures present about what had happened during the highly unusual proceeding. Wosik, who would have to face the voters, needed the support of the Chicago machine to be reelected. David Hamlin commented, "[A] cynical observer would suggest that there was a direct relationship between the case, the judge, the sheriff's telephone call, and the outcome of the hearing."

Harvey Schwartz didn't think Elrod's phone call made any difference. Judge Wosik was on Skokie's side from the outset. "I had a hard time containing the judge. The judge was running away with my case," Schwartz recalled.

> He let the ACLU lawyers know in no uncertain terms that he, Joe Wosik, had served in the United States Army, that he had served in the European theatre, he had seen what the Nazis did, and the crimes against humanity—against Jews and Poles—he had relatives, family, in Poland—Warsaw—other places where the Nazis were out. . . . I had all I had to do to restrain Wosik. He wasn't about to be restrained. His face was red and he was sitting on the edge of his chair and he was staring down. Days and weeks and months later he would always tell me that I was too easy on them—too easy on those Nazis and their sympathizers, and as much as say, "You probably never would have gotten an injunction from another judge because you just didn't do a good enough job." . . . He didn't need phone calls from anybody.

The record seems to validate Schwartz's view. Before the full argument over the injunction sought by Skokie began, Goldberger followed usual procedure by moving to dismiss the Skokie case. He described the proposed demonstration as one that would "occur in an orderly fashion in front of the Village Hall for a period of between 20 to 30 minutes on a Sunday afternoon" and, referring to the injunction sought, added, "Such an order, whatever we might feel about the content of that speech, violates the very essence of the First Amendment." The only basis for prior restraint established by *Brandenburg v. Ohio*, he stated, was that "the conduct will be unlawful." The village of Skokie had not even alleged that, he said, and cited the Pentagon Papers case—the case in which the Court had declined to allow the federal government to restrain the *New York Times'* publication of the Defense Department report on the history of the American involvement in the Vietnam War.

Wosik's reply was straightforward:

> I do not have to expound theories of nazism. . . . [T]his Court has a most unusual situation here. . . . I have here a Village with a great number of Jewish people. I have here before me a group of citizens of this country who endured, suffered, and God knows what happened to their respective families. . . . I can take into judicial notice the Nuremberg trials [the post–World War II international tribunal at which Nazi leaders were convicted of crimes against humanity] and what a court of law found.

With that, Wosik denied the motion to dismiss.

Whatever his motivation, as soon as the two attorneys rested their case Wosik held that the pamphlets the NSPA had distributed in Skokie were intended to incite riot and cause bodily harm. "There is no need for me to go on with any impressions other than this evidence," he said, adding that the pamphlets were meant to do "all those things that the Constitution does not give a defendant a right to do." He therefore granted an injunction prohibiting the party

> from engaging in any of the following acts on May 1, 1977, within the Village of Skokie: Marching, walking or parading in the uniform of the National Socialist Party of America; Marching, walking or parading or otherwise displaying the swastika on or off their person; Distributing pamphlets or displaying any materials which incite or promote hatred against persons of Jewish faith or ancestry or hatred against persons of any faith or ancestry, race or religion.

A few reporters were present for the argument. A television crew, waiting outside the courtroom to interview the Nazi leader, got shots of both Collin and Goldberger. The crew immediately sent its footage to the television station. Hamlin recalled that subsequent television programs about Skokie would be announced by "trailers" saying things such as "Nazis March on Skokie, Details at Ten." He, Goldberger, and O'Toole returned to the ACLU office to discover that its switchboard was lit up, all eight telephone lines taking calls from people outraged at the idea of the ACLU defending the Nazis. These were only the first of hundreds of calls that would swamp the ACLU lines during the next year. But, as Hamlin wrote in 1980, not one of the callers knew what the Nazis proposed to do in Skokie. All of them assumed the Nazis were planning to march through the village.

In fact, as Collin's letters to Skokie officials had indicated all along, the NSPA intended to have demonstrators walk single file in front of the village hall, rather like workers on strike. The party had no plan to march in the survivors' neighborhoods. It would not parade in front of their homes or march past their synagogues. It would confine itself to the downtown business district in which the village hall was located. As Barbara O'Toole would say two decades later, "There was never going to be a march. It was always walking back and forth in front of the village hall."

The reaction to the Nazis' plan clearly revealed the difference between the word "march" and the word "demonstrate." When the case hit the rest of the Chicago media the morning after it was presented in Judge Wosik's courtroom, some spoke of a proposed march "in" Skokie; others referred to a march "through" Skokie. Judge Wosik himself enjoined any "march." On occasion, the press referred to a "rally" in Skokie, conjuring up the image of loud anti-Semitic speeches. Much of the debate about the case that raged in the United States from April 1977 through July 1978 was based on a stunning misconception.

The misconception echoes through all the court opinions generated by the controversy. And Collin encouraged it, clearly delighted at all the publicity and by the frantic fears of Skokie's Jewish community. After all, a "march *through* Skokie" had the ring of a large and threatening mass of people, rather than of two or three dozen people picketing in front of the village hall. Whether positive or negative, media coverage was Collin's major goal, and the media were all too willing to help him achieve it.

The federal court system and each state court system has its own hierarchical scheme. All of them include a trial level, at least one appellate level, and a court of last resort. In Illinois, a party dissatisfied with a decision by a circuit court can appeal the decision to the Illinois Appellate Court. Goldberger turned to it the day after Judge Wosik's ruling, asking the court to stay (put off) Judge Wosik's injunction until the case could be thoroughly argued before it. Late on the afternoon of April 30, the appellate court denied the request without writing an opinion. It was Friday, the Chicago business district was closing down for the weekend, and Goldberger left for home on the assumption that nothing more would happen before he appealed the appellate court's decision to the Illinois Supreme Court. But Collin had other plans.

His demonstration was planned for May 1, and Judge Wosik had of course enjoined the NSPA from demonstrating in Skokie on that day. Collin had learned to read legal writs that concerned him, however, and he thought he could get around this one. On the afternoon of April 29, after the appellate court denied his petition for a stay, Collin made an announcement: the NSPA would demonstrate in Skokie on April 30, the very next day.

Collin clearly thought he could outwit Judge Wosik and gain additional media attention. His legal coup would result in even more publicity for his demonstration than it might otherwise have gotten. If his sole goal was to demonstrate, he would not have gone before the television cameras to announce the demonstration in advance and given Skokie's residents the chance to organize. If he considered the possibility of a counterdemonstration taking place as a result of his announcement, he no doubt welcomed the prospect as adding to the drama. But Skokie's dismay was to have results beyond a counterdemonstration.

Phones were ringing again in Skokie that night of Friday, April 29. This time the calls were from its Holocaust survivors, spreading the news of the demonstration newly scheduled for Saturday at noon. By nine o'clock the next morning, Skokie residents had begun to gather near the village hall. So had several left-wing groups from Chicago, carrying with them four-foot-long stakes studded with nails and a flyer headlined, "No Free Speech for Fascists." Others in the throng carried signs with slogans such as "Never Again Dachau" and "Never Again Treblinka." By noon the crowd had grown to many hundreds.

Skokie's elected officials huddled in an emergency consultation earlier that morning. The result was a telephone call to the home of Harold Sullivan, another Cook County Circuit Court judge, who lived in Skokie. The village lawyers wanted to see him in order to ask that the injunction be modified to read "without limitation as to date or time" rather than "May 1." Sullivan agreed to hear the village. Of course, according to legal procedure in the United States, each side would have to be given a chance to present its case. Skokie officials later claimed that they called Goldberger at the ACLU office in Chicago to tell him about the hastily scheduled hearing but got no reply. Goldberger said he was in the office all morning, working, and that no such phone call had come in. Former Illinois ACLU board president Franklyn Haiman could attest that Goldberger had been at the office and answering telephone calls. Goldberger, too busy to be in Skokie for the demonstration, had asked Haiman to monitor the situation. Haiman stayed in touch with him from a public telephone across the street from the village hall.

Whatever the truth of the matter, Judge Sullivan altered the injunction in the absence of any representation of Collin, effectively banning the demonstration. He was persuaded that Collin's appearance would lead to violence and issued an emergency injunction subject to Judge Wosik's review when the courts reopened on Monday, May 2.

The ACLU was unaware of that; so was Collin. He and a group of six or seven cars carrying his followers were already on their way from Chicago to Skokie. They got as far as the Skokie exit on Edens Expressway. There they were met by a police car and informed of the new ruling, at which point they turned their cars around and went back to Chicago. As Collin insisted throughout the matter, he had no wish to break the law. His deference to law may well have been the result of an assessment that it was the safest position to take rather than of a principled commitment to law—safest because it would both ensure him police protection and keep him out of the Cook County Jail, whose black population he feared—but nonetheless he maintained it. From the time of his first letter to the Skokie Park District and throughout the months that followed, Collin broke no law.

With the immediate crisis averted that Saturday morning, Skokie officials announced to the crowd at the village hall that the Nazis were not coming to Skokie after all. The survivors reacted with disbelief. If Collin could get around the law through a technicality, anything was possible. Perhaps the injunction had not been altered; perhaps it had not really been served. People were still milling around the hall as the clock struck 2 P.M.

Harvey Schwartz was one of the officials who stood, that day, on the balcony that jutted out from the village hall's second floor, watching the crowd gathered below. The sight changed his attitude toward the dispute. "When I observed these survivors—you could tell who they were—some of them I knew," he said, "I began to have a different feeling about the First Amendment." He saw them "standing there, some of them in almost a catatonic state—petrified—shaking—crying." While many were angry and shouting, those were not the people who impressed Schwartz the most. It was the others, trembling at the thought of "those swastikas and brown shirts and boots and Nazi insignia" that were "more like a physical assault than an exchange of ideas." That was the moment when Schwartz "began to see this whole event in a different light."

It was a reaction shared by many people in Skokie and elsewhere. City manager John Matzer and a member of the village council both told scholar Donald Downs, who did extensive interviews for his book *Nazis in Skokie*, that the counterdemonstration was a turning point for them, too. "I didn't appreciate the psychological effect until now," Downs quotes Matzer as saying. "There is no question that for survivors it was a reliving of the whole thing, and I changed my attitude." Letters published in newspapers all over the country during the next year, and particularly in the Chicago area, would argue that free speech was all very well but that Skokie, with its survivor residents, was a special case. Some insisted that First Amendment protections were perverted if they were extended to those who would deny the speech of others. The survivors' pain seemingly was felt by people throughout the United States.

It was the survivors' anguish that put the Skokie case in a category unlike other free speech situations. That, at any rate, was the argument most widely used for keeping the NSPA from demonstrating there. The *Chicago Tribune* asked Mayor Smith and the ACLU's David Hamlin to contribute opinion pieces for its January 1, 1978, edition. "The situation in the Village of Skokie is unique in the history of the United States and indeed in the history of the world," Smith wrote.

Nowhere else do victims of the Nazi Holocaust constitute 10 per cent of the total population of a community. Nowhere else would a march of Nazis in storm trooper uniforms carrying the hated swastika constitute a deliberate provocation and a cynical taunt. Nowhere else would this proscribed Nazi march evoke in so many people such vivid memories of the manner in which their loved ones met their death.

To Smith, "the circumstances presented in the Nazi assault upon Skokie" made the case an unusual one from the standpoint of the First Amendment: "Just as the Constitution does not preserve the right of the Nazis to physically assault the Holocaust survivors in Skokie, so should it not license them to perpetrate an infinitely more serious assault upon their sensibilities."

Skokie moved to alleviate the survivors' concerns two days after the Nazis were turned away from the village—the same day that Judge Wosik extended his injunction. The reaction of Goldstein and the others, the depth of their fear and hostility, initially had come as a surprise to Skokie officials, but now the local government was convinced that a court decree would not be seen as a sufficient response. It felt that it finally understood the survivors' reaction and that their reaction had to take precedence over the Nazis' alleged First Amendment rights. Some officials were convinced that if the Nazis came to Skokie, violence was inevitable. They also were tired of being on the defensive, of reacting to Collin or the courts. On May 2, at its regularly scheduled weekly meeting, the village council adopted three new ordinances designed to keep the Nazis out of Skokie for all time.

The statutes were drafted by Gilbert Gordon, assistant corporate counsel of Skokie and Schwartz's second in command. Ordinance 994, "An Ordinance Relating to Parades and Public Assemblies," was written as a traffic and safety law designed to protect Skokie residents "from disruption of essential services, such as fire protection, program participation, and the orderly pursuit of their activities" and to safeguard their health, safety, and welfare. It regulated public assemblies that reasonably could be expected to involve over fifty people. Demonstrators now had to obtain a permit from the village at least thirty days in advance, posting public liability insurance of $300,000 and property damage insurance of $50,000. The village manager was given the job of issuing permits and was directed to hand them out only when the contemplated activity would not "create an imminent danger of a substantial breach of the peace, riot, or similar disorder." He had to feel certain that the demonstration would not "portray criminality, depravity, or lack of virtue" in any "person or group of persons by reason of reference to religious, racial, ethnic, national or regional affiliation." The ACLU would argue that the permit requirement, allowing the village manager to decide which speech was permissible before it took place, constituted a prior restraint.

No permit was required for school-sponsored activities or "normal or scheduled activities of the Village," meaning that public assemblies cosponsored by the village government were exempted from the permit requirement. In addition, any provision of the ordinance could be waived by the mayor and the village council—permitting them to pick and choose among proposed public assemblies. The usual approach to insurance requirements such as those in Ordinance 994 is for groups, which rarely have a cash flow sufficient to post the requisite amount of insurance themselves, to secure a bond from an insurance company. The companies in turn provide what amounts to a short-term insurance bond for a relatively small fee. No one doubted that groups such as the NSPA would find it impossible to obtain such insurance and thus would be unable to hold public demonstrations. In fact, a licensed insurance broker eventually would testify in federal court that her attempt to get such coverage for the NSPA in Chicago and Skokie was unsuccessful, in spite of her working on the matter over a period of six months and contacting thirteen different insurance companies. While the ordinance enabled the mayor and village council to waive the insurance requirement, no criteria for a waiver were included in the statute. The mayor and council thus enacted a law that gave themselves the sole power to decide what groups' speech could be heard on the streets of Skokie, waiving the insurance requirement for speech they liked and imposing it only on speech that they found offensive.

According to Ordinance 994, permits could not be issued for public assemblies that intended to engage in activities prohibited by the accompanying Ordinance 995. An "Ordinance Prohibiting the Dissemination of Materials Which Promote and Incite Group Hatred," 995 made it a criminal offense to display or disseminate any material "which promotes and incites hatred against persons by reason of their race, national origin, or religion" or to wear "markings and clothing of symbolic significance" that would have the same effect. Gordon and Schwartz assumed this would be found constitutional under the *Beauharnais* group libel doctrine. (The ordinances were similar to the Illinois statute upheld in that case—which, however, had been repealed by Illinois in 1964.) Goldberger and O'Toole would argue that it was the kind of language that would have prevented antisegregationists from demonstrating.

It was followed by Ordinance 996, "An Ordinance Prohibiting Demonstrations by Members of Political Parties Wearing Military-Style Uniforms," which said in part, "No person shall engage in any march, walk or public demonstration as a member or on behalf of any political party while wearing a military-style uniform." The reason for the prohibition, according to the preamble, was that demonstrations by party members in military-style uniforms were "repugnant to the tradition of civilian control of government" as well as to "the standards of morality and decency of the people of the Village of Skokie." A political party was defined as "an organization existing primarily to influence and deal with the structure or affairs of government, politics or the state." Collin's group, it will be remembered, called itself the National Socialist *Party* of America, and the ordinance clearly was directed at the NSPA. But, as a federal judge would point out, the law would prohibit members of the American Legion from marching in uniform to support Republican or Democratic party candidates.

All three ordinances were adopted unanimously. Anything else was hardly to be expected, given the high feelings aroused by the controversy. Donald Downs quotes village board member Charles Conrad as saying that "if I had voted 'no,' my chances of re-election would have been slim or none"—an indication of where the electorate stood on the matter. The new laws were to have at least one unexpected consequence. A group of Jewish war veterans discovered a few months later that the ordinances prevented them from demonstrating against Collin in their uniforms. The village manager subsequently granted permits for a "Walk With Israel" sponsored by the Jewish Community Centers, the Masada Torch Relay organized by the Youth Movement of the Zionist Organization of Chicago, and the Niles East High School and Niles North High School homecoming parades. The village cosponsored the American Legion's annual Poppy Day parade, so the ordinances did not apply to it and the Legion's uniforms did not come under scrutiny; and it permitted a march by the Veterans of Foreign Wars (presumably permitted to march with uniforms by a finding that the definition of "political party" did not apply to them).

When the Illinois ACLU board of directors met on May 4 to decide whether it wanted to continue its representation of Collin, it had before it both Judge Wosik's amended injunction and the three new Skokie ordinances. The large number of members present at the meeting heard Edwin Rothschild, the board's president, describe the events of Skokie. He added his belief that to reverse his and the staff's decision to represent Collin would be to deny the cardinal principle for which the ACLU stood: the right of all citizens to express their ideas and be heard by whichever of their fellow citizens chose to listen. Board members expressed their extreme distaste for Collin and his views but, after some discussion, voted unanimously to go ahead with the case.

Goldberger and O'Toole quickly filed papers with the Illinois Supreme Court, asking it to grant a stay of Judge Wosik's injunction and to hear the case on an expedited basis. Formally, the case was still before the Illinois Appellate Court, which had refused to hear an expedited argument about it but had not yet decided the case on the merits. The state supreme court would have to grant permission if the case was to be placed on its own docket. A few years earlier, the case of *Organization for a Better Austin v. Keefe* (1971), which concerned prior restraint on speech, had taken three years to move through the Illinois courts and up to the federal Supreme Court. The two lawyers believed that length of time constituted an unacceptable prior restraint. Nonetheless, as a procedural matter they had to go through the state supreme court. The court, as anticipated, told them to complete proceedings before the appellate court and declined to stay the injunction during the time it took for the case to reach the top of the appellate court's calendar. At that point they turned to their last hope, the United States Supreme Court.

The federal court system in the United States is divided into eleven "circuits" that each cover a number of states in a part of the country and a separate circuit for the District of Columbia. Each circuit in turn is formally headed by one of the justices on the Supreme Court, with whom emergency petitions are filed. The Seventh Circuit covers Illinois, Indiana, and Wisconsin. The justice with responsibility for the Seventh Circuit in 1977 was John Paul Stevens. The only person to be appointed to the Supreme Court by President Gerald Ford, Stevens had taken his seat in mid-December 1975. He was still the junior justice on the Court in 1977.

Stevens was a former private practitioner and professor of antitrust law at Northwestern and the University of Chicago law schools. Before joining the Supreme Court he served for five years on the Seventh Circuit Court of Appeals, where he developed a reputation for short, frank, finely crafted opinions. June 1977 was too early for an assessment of Stevens's position on free speech or his likely attitude toward Collin's plea, but the Court's rules permitted no "judge shopping": Goldberger had to deliver the plea for a stay of the injunction to the justice in charge of the Seventh Circuit.

Instead of dealing with the matter alone, as would have been usual for petitions to a justice in his capacity as supervisor of a circuit, Justice Stevens treated the application as a petition for certiorari—a place on the Supreme Court's docket. Most nonemergency cases decided by the Court follow a schedule of petition for certiorari, an answering petition by the other side, a granting of certiorari by the Court, the filing of written briefs by both parties, and oral argument. After the court reaches its preliminary decision, one justice writes an opinion for the majority of justices, with any justice who chooses to write a concurring or dissenting opinion free to do so. This time the procedure was different. Whether because he was outraged by the case or because, as the Court's junior justice, he wanted the input of his colleagues, Stevens took the matter to the entire bench of nine justices. They both granted the case an immediate place on the Court's docket and, with only Goldberger and O'Toole's papers and Skokie's reply before them, decided upon its merits. Goldberger and O'Toole knew nothing about this until, to their total surprise, the clerk of the Court called on June 14 to tell them that a decision had been made.

The Court issued its ruling per curiam. Such opinions traditionally are very brief, the implication being that the decision is such an obvious one that it requires no extended explanation. The first of only three paragraphs in *National Socialist Party of America v. Village of Skokie* was written in Justice Stevens's terse style. (The names of the parties had been reversed because it was the NSPA that was appealing the case and the plaintiff's name appears first.) The first paragraph summarized the history of the injunction handed down by Judge Wosik and denied speedy review by the Illinois appellate and supreme courts. The Court's majority went on to reverse the Illinois Supreme Court's denial of a stay of the injunction, saying that the injunction would deprive the appellants of rights protected by the First Amendment. Review by the appellate courts might, "in the normal course . . . take a year or more to complete." That, the Court said, was too long when First Amendment rights were involved. A state seeking to impose a prior restraint had to provide "immediate appellate review." Where no such review was available, the state had to issue a stay of the injunction. The Illinois Supreme Court was ordered to arrange for a hearing at once. As Goldberger later said, the Court had taken his petition and Skokie's reply and "treated the legal issue as one which was so clear that it could be decided summarily in our client's favor."

Suddenly, the case was front-page news across the nation. Journalists and television commentators reported excitedly that the Supreme Court, in a highly unusual expedited hearing, had taken Collin's side in the dispute.

The Court of course had done no such thing. Like the ACLU, it made no statement about the acceptability or value of Collin's message. Instead, it had emphasized that the right to due process—the right not to be deprived of rights in the absence of proper procedure—could not be abridged. It said that what was at issue was Collin's First Amendment right to free speech and that his claim had to be given an immediate hearing.

Justice William H. Rehnquist, writing for himself, Chief Justice Warren E. Burger, and Justice Potter Stewart, dissented, on the grounds that the state courts had not yet decided the case on its merits—which, ironically enough, was exactly Goldberger's complaint. In his dissent, however, Rehnquist indicated that he expected the Illinois appellate courts at a minimum to modify the injunction substantially. It appeared that the three dissenters disagreed with what they viewed as the Court's overly hasty action rather than with the majority's assertion that the right of speech was at issue, with the implication being that at the least the injunction was unacceptably broad. Justice Byron R. White voted to deny the stay but wrote no opinion.

Collin's right to express his views in Skokie—or, as the media had it, to march or parade *through* Skokie—became a matter for hot debate around the country. Both the Court and the ACLU were widely seen as overly formalistic on the constitutional issue and unsympathetic to the survivors' distress. The Jewish Defense League, an organization originally created to safeguard Jewish neighborhoods in New York City, burst into ACLU national headquarters and staged a sit-in. One member of the group spat on Executive Director Aryeh Neier as the group left after several hours. (At almost the same time, the New York ACLU affiliate, based in New York City and as insistent on the right to speak as other ACLU entities, was defending the right of the JDL to picket in front of the offices of the Soviet mission to the United Nations.) The JDL and an offshoot also held sit-ins in ACLU offices in Los Angeles and Florida. A group of self-styled antifascists took over the Illinois ACLU office for about an hour, plopping themselves on the staff's desks. Collin, basking in the publicity, announced himself as "very pleased" at the Supreme Court's ruling "because the more this case is dragged out, the more publicity and attention we get."

The person who took the full fury of the response was David Goldberger.

Barbara O'Toole, who did much of her work in the case at home, preferred to remain in the background and leave most media involvement to Goldberger and David Hamlin. That decision was to have the effect of protecting her from the kind of personal abuse that Hamlin, also a non-Jew, received. He was repeatedly insulted and lambasted by Jews who considered it offensive for a non-Jew to be involved in a cause that was highly upsetting to them. He described the letters he received from a man who wrote that "he would have called me an S.O.B. except that he knew that I didn't have a mother." Tired of endless arguments about Skokie, Hamlin hid behind his newspaper as he took the commuter train from Evanston to Chicago each day. Frank Haiman, the Illinois ACLU board member who had been its president from 1964 to 1975, also made numerous public appearances to explain the ACLU's position. He did so not because he expected to win audiences to the ACLU's side but because it was his impression that about half of the people in the audiences to which he spoke could be moved from a hostile to a neutral position, accepting his argument about the free speech principle. The people in the other half, however, were vocal and more. Haiman would recall their response as being exemplified by the Cleveland, Ohio, rabbi who swung at Haiman's nose—and almost connected—to demonstrate his reaction to the use of the free speech doctrine on behalf of the NSPA. On another occasion, when Haiman spoke at a B'nai B'rith lodge in a town near Skokie, an elderly survivor stood up, shouting epithets, ending by shrieking that Haiman didn't deserve to live. The very large B'nai B'rith officer running the meeting quickly adjourned it and offered to walk Haiman to his car, for which a shaky Haiman was extremely grateful. One of the rare occasions he received support occurred after he spoke in another synagogue, where a woman with a Jewish Star of David around her neck asked the hostile rabbi whether the rabbi's position that the NSPA should stay out of neighborhoods would apply equally to her if she walked through an anti-Semitic area wearing her star. The rabbi, he recalled, harumphed; the audience broke up.

But large parts of both the general public and the national bar considered Goldberger to be the real villain of the piece. They had no compunctions about telling him so.

An attorney in the case that would later be brought by Sol Goldstein referred to Goldberger in a court document as "neo-Nazi counsel." His parents heard their son denounced in synagogue by their rabbi. He was called a Nazi sympathizer or a Nazi dupe when he spoke in public. A group in Gary, Indiana, attempted to present him with a "Nazi of the Year" award when he spoke in a synagogue there. One of the more civilized of the angry letters he received said, "I wish you one month in a concentration camp, surrounded by swastikas." Another correspondent expressed a different wish, writing, "May God strike you and your family dead." When Goldberger spoke at a Convocation on Free Speech organized by the ACLU in 1978, he was asked by an angry woman, "Would you defend the Nazis if they wanted to march in your neighborhood?" "Defending them," he replied, "*is* like having them march in my neighborhood." Donald Downs interviewed survivors who considered Goldberger to be the equivalent of European collaborators with the Nazis. Pulitzer Prize–winning journalist

J. Anthony Lukas described Goldberger as subjected to "torrents of abuse" and the Skokie case as having changed his life.

Goldberger was appalled at the lack of support from individual lawyers and from the organized bar. He lamented what he saw as their failure to stand by two principles: the right to speech and the obligation of attorneys, codified in the American Bar Association's 1969 Code of Professional Responsibility, to represent parties even when "a client or cause is unpopular or community action is adverse." Most of the lawyers with whom Goldberger spoke disagreed, saying that the ACLU should have left the Nazis unrepresented and unpublicized. Several resigned from the Illinois ACLU as soon as they heard of the affiliate's involvement in the case. An ACLU letter sent to a large number of Chicago criminal defense lawyers, in the hope that they would support the decision to provide representation in an unpopular case, brought only silence. To Goldberger's dismay, former United States attorney general Edward Levi, now a private lawyer in Chicago, declined to put his name on a public statement urging people not to abandon the ACLU. Levi said the reason was that he was not an ACLU member. A local criminal court judge commented privately that even the criminal defense bar found Goldberger's client too noxious. When a partner at a large Chicago law firm helped Goldberger and O'Toole with some of the paperwork in the case they eventually brought in federal district court (*Collin v. Smith*, discussed below), he conditioned his aid on neither his name or that of his firm being used. Goldberger later commented that the lawyer "was legimately worried about damage that publicity might do."

Ironically enough, one of the few non-ACLU lawyers to understand Goldberger's position was his opponent Harvey Schwartz. Two decades later Schwartz would say about Goldberger, "He was put through Hell. He was doing what he was supposed to do . . . he was standing up for what he felt the ACLU was all about. He was a tragic figure. The Jewish community [in Skokie and Chicago] came down on him so heavily." When they were both on the speakers' circuit, Schwartz said, it was clear that Goldberger was fighting a hopeless battle for public understanding. Audiences were so hostile to Goldberger that Schwartz frequently considered him to be in need of physical protection.

The Supreme Court's ruling generated national interest in Goldberger and Skokie and Collin. Its corollary result was to add vituperation from people around the country to the epithets David Goldberger was already receiving from the Chicago area. The worst, however, was yet to come.

On June 22, the Illinois Supreme Court responded to the United States Supreme Court's order, telling the Illinois Appellate Court either to hold an immediate appellate hearing about Judge Wosik's injunction or to issue a stay of it. The appellate court set July 7 as the last date for submission of briefs and July 8 for oral argument. With his usual gleeful flair for publicity, Collin immediately announced he would demonstrate in Skokie on the Fourth of July.

CHAPTER 5

Speech, Symbols, and Suffering

If any appreciable number of persons are inclined to advocate murder on principle,
I should wish them to state their opinions openly and fearlessly, because I should think
that the shortest way of exploding the principle and of ascertaining the true causes
of such a perversion of moral sentiment.

LESLIE STEPHEN, *The Suppression of Poisonous Opinions* (1883)

Collin wrote to Skokie that the July 4 demonstration would follow his earlier plan. Thirty to fifty people in uniforms and swastikas, carrying placards about the right to free speech, would participate in a demonstration that would last for about half an hour. There would be no disruption of traffic. Collin requested a waiver of the $350,000 insurance requirement or, if that was not possible, the help of Skokie in obtaining insurance. John Matzer, the village manager, replied as anticipated: the demonstration could not take place because the NSPA's military-style uniforms would violate Ordinance 996. There were two obstacles to the NSPA demonstration: the injunction issued by Judge Wosik, which was not scheduled to be examined by the Illinois Appellate Court until July 8, and the three ordinances. The stage was set for the next legal round.

Goldberger and O'Toole began it by bringing suit on Collin's behalf in late June in the federal district court located in Chicago, asking that the three ordinances be invalidated as violations of the First Amendment and that an injunction be issued both against their enforcement and against any further efforts by Skokie to prevent the NSPA from exercising its First Amendment rights there *(Collin v. Smith)*. The case was pending when the Midwest office of the Anti-Defamation League (ADL), aided by the Chicago Jewish Federation's public affairs committee, of which Sol Goldstein was a member, began its own lawsuit. (The Midwest ADL's action would be endorsed by the national ADL's civil rights committee in November.)

The ADL's case was a class action suit brought on behalf of Goldstein and the other Skokie survivors, asking the Cook County Circuit Court to issue a permanent injunction barring Collin from marching in Skokie "while wearing or displaying Nazi insignia" *(Goldstein v. Collin)*. The case came as a surprise because the organization had argued until then that demonstrations by Nazis should be ignored and that anything that resulted in Collin's receiving more publicity should be avoided. The suit, however, relied upon the concept of "menticide," defined by the ADL's lawyer in the case as the deliberate infliction of severe mental and emotional distress. "Menticide" was in fact a term created for the case by lead attorney Jerome Torshen, who argued that the sight of the Nazis would inflict "menticide" on the survivors. (It was Torshen who would refer to Goldberger as a "neo-Nazi lawyer."As a result of outraged protests from Aryeh Neier at the national ACLU office, the ADL ordered Torshen to withdraw the epithet.) Torshen based his approach on the tort (a wrong done by one person to another, and legally actionable) of intentional infliction of emotional harm. His theory was that Collin intended to inflict emotional harm on the survivors by reviving their memories of their horrific experiences under the Nazis.

By the end of June 1977 there were three cases pending simultaneously in the Skokie situation, and the reader may feel the need here for a road map. The first case was *Skokie v. NSPA*, now labeled *NSPA v. Skokie* for some purposes, in which the village had sued for an injunction against the demonstration. Judge Wosik had ruled in favor of Skokie; the Illinois appellate and supreme courts had declined to issue a stay of his order while it was being appealed; the United States Supreme Court had ordered the Illinois Supreme Court to see either that the stay was granted or that the case was heard quickly, and the Illinois Appellate Court had consequently set a date for oral argument. *Collin v. Smith*, the case in which Collin attacked the constitutionality of the three ordinances, had been filed in federal district court and was yet to be heard. Finally, *Goldstein v. Collin* was Goldstein and the ADL's attempt to have the demonstration enjoined on the basis of potential menticide.

The ADL submitted an affidavit in *Goldstein v. Collin* detailing the history of the Nazi Party in Germany and what the ADL expected the effect on the survivors to be if they were exposed to what they would see as a reenactment of the Holocaust era. Another affidavit for Goldstein was submitted by David Gutmann, a psychologist at Northwestern University who volunteered his services. Gutmann had been a merchant seaman during World War II. After the war, he served as a volunteer sailor for the Haganah, the Jewish underground in Palestine, which attempted to smuggle in Jewish

Holocaust survivors. The British, then in control of Palestine, limited immigration by Jews. Gutmann testified that he was captured twice, serving time in the British fortress of Acre in Palestine and in the British prison camp on Cyprus. He asserted that a victim of racism internalized racist slurs and "polluted his inner experience of himself." The "outer insult," Gutmann told the court, would "become an inner accusation" that could no longer be "evaded," and the victim's self-concept would be seriously affected. That would be the case even if Collin appeared in a business suit, now that Collin had been identified with the Nazi Party. Gutmann equated the use of the word "Jew" by a Nazi with falsely shouting fire in a crowded theater.

On the morning of June 29, the first legal jousting in the Goldstein case took place in Chicago's Daley Center, when Goldberger tried unsuccessfully to have the circuit court dismiss the Goldstein suit. Judge Archibald Carey, an African American former alderman with a solid record on civil rights issues, set the trial in the case for August 29.

Both parties have a right to "depose," or question, possible witnesses before trial. Goldberger naturally deposed Sol Goldstein. Under oath, Goldstein reported that he had in fact seen Collin in Nazi uniform, having gone to some of Collin's demonstrations in Chicago long before the NSPA had any plans about Skokie. The obvious question was why Goldstein objected to a sight he had deliberately sought out not many years earlier.

The answer, to Goldstein, was just as clear. There was a difference to him between going to see a Nazi march elsewhere and having that Nazi demonstrate in his home town. In addition, the suit was a class action, brought on behalf of all survivors in Skokie. Most if not all of the others had never seen Collin in person.

Goldstein's argument raised a complicated legal question. By bringing a class action on behalf of himself and all others similarly situated, was Goldstein claiming that all Skokie survivors would be harmed by the sight of the NSPA? If so, presumably every survivor had to be present at the demonstration in order to be harmed. If that was not the case, then the survivors' physical presence at the demonstration seemingly was not necessary, as they would be hurt by the fact of the demonstration's taking place. If, then, the claim was that mere knowledge of the Nazis' visibility in Skokie caused the kind of severe harm contemplated in the "fighting words" doctrine, wasn't it equally logical to ban photographs of Nazis in uniform or the miniseries NBC was then showing on the Holocaust and to prohibit the Skokie public library from owning and circulating illustrated books about the Nazi era? Skokie counsel Harvey Schwartz was to say, "The presence of these symbols [the swastika] was literally an assault." Did a television program about World War II constitute the same kind of an assault? If not, what was the legal basis for differentiating it? Could a similar argument have been used to keep the raised fist, the symbol of the Black Power movement, out of the South during the days of the civil rights movement? Could it now be used to prevent Black Power marchers from demonstrating there, because of possible "menticide" suffered by some white southerners, or to censor television programs about slavery, because of possible "menticide" inflicted upon some black southerners?

The majority of people in Skokie were not interested in the abstract argument. A typed four-paragraph form letter to city manager Matzer was reproduced in large quantities and sent to his office by many citizens. Dated June 25, 1977, it said, "We are very fearful that there will be bloodshed and violence (possible death) if the Nazis are allowed to march in Skokie, Illinois on the July 4th weekend." "It isn't a matter of freedom of speech," the letter went on, "it is a matter of danger of loss of life and also injury to many people." A space was left for protesters to add Matzer's name and address and their own.

Feelings in Skokie were running very high in any event, and there were those who deliberately fed the tension. Meir Kahane, leader of the Jewish Defense League, said upon his arrival in Skokie on June 22, "We intend to bloody the Nazis should they try [to demonstrate there]. I am not predicting violence—I am promising violence." On June 29 he told a standing-room-only meeting of 350 people at Congregation B'nai Emunah, "If I see a Nazi marching, I will break his head. . . . We spit in the graves of 6,000,000 Jews if we allow the Nazis to march." He would not react alone, he told his listeners; the JDL was planning to pay the expenses of 800 people who would travel to Skokie from all over the country in order to join in. He added to loud applause, referring to the argument in the *Goldstein* case that the NSPA had a right to speak in Skokie, "Rights? They have rights? What person has the right to demand that others be put into ovens?"

The tension was fueled as well by people who felt more directly involved. That morning, outside Judge Carey's courtroom, Collin had been confronted by a seventy-four-year-old man who later told the media that seven of his cousins had been killed in the Holocaust. The man raged at Collin, "I'd like to crack your skull. That's how to deal with a snake." Another man, a Skokie resident, had shouted to television reporters, "Hitler started with a couple of jerks like this in a saloon. I fought in the Pacific during World War II. I'm old enough to remember what took place."

Like Kahane, Collin claimed to be mustering supporters, and said that he expected Nazi "storm troopers" from California, Missouri, New Jersey, Nebraska, Ohio, and Texas to attend his demonstration. He reiterated his statement that the NSPA had singled out Skokie "because it's a Jew suburb." ADL representative Abbot Rosen, whose organization was sponsoring the Goldstein case, was sufficiently concerned by the calls for violence to tell the media, "This matter is just where it should be—in the courts. Advocating force to stop the march would be disastrous." Rabbi Laurence Montrose of the Skokie Central Traditional Synagogue, who was widely considered to be the survivors' unofficial chaplain, wrote to his congregation's 640 families that it was their "solemn duty" to counterdemonstrate peacefully. The survivors responded on June 30, holding a large demonstration that emphasized the seriousness of their concerns.

A panel presentation on the issue had been held in a Skokie synagogue toward the end of June. The panel consisted of David Hamlin, Skokie assistant counsel Gilbert Gordon, an ADL representative, and a Holocaust survivor. It was shortly before the panel discussion was to take place that Hamlin received the call warning him that he would not leave Skokie alive. The ADL representative stated that he still believed the best way to handle the situation was for the community to allow the demonstration but then either ignore it or stage a counterdemonstration. He was roundly booed. Some weeks later, at a debate between the ACLU's David Hamlin and Jerome Torshen, Hamlin told the Skokie audience, "The course that I would have advocated would have been to have had the anti-Nazi persons lined up on the side of the street at the time Frank Collin showed up."

Torshen rejected the suggestion. Speaking of the threatening telephone calls being received by Skokie survivors, he said he had told the ACLU he would hold it "personally responsible" for the calls and promised to rip its phones out if the calls didn't stop. "How I'd accomplish that is my business," Torshen continued. "That's part of being a lawyer—you sometimes learn how to do things. You have to help yourself."

Hamlin protested, "We don't tell Frank Collin who to call or who not to call. . . . The notion that ACLU is responsible for what the Nazis do, or in effect for Nazism itself, if fallacious and unfair."

"I think a lawyer has the obligation to control his client," Torshen replied to applause. The citizens of Skokie were not in a mood for restraint.

On the weekend of Saturday, July 2, Collin held what he called a "National Socialist Convention," a meeting attended by Nazi "leaders" from around the country. Collin told reporters Saturday morning that thirty people were present. He introduced several of them at a press conference outside the party's Chicago headquarters, while about one hundred placard-carrying members of groups such as the Committee Against Racism and the Progressive Labor Party demonstrated in protest. Fighting broke out. One of the police officers present was injured, as were four other people. Perhaps that, and the turmoil in Skokie, persuaded the NSPA that it might be dangerous to demonstrate in Skokie just then. Collin must have been aware that although the Supreme Court had stayed Wosik's injunction, the three Skokie ordinances were still in force. Under them, each NSPA demonstrator could be fined $500 three times for demonstrating—once for demonstrating without a permit, once for disseminating material promoting group hatred, and once for demonstrating in a military-style uniform—and would no doubt be sentenced to the six-month prison terms permitted by Ordinances 995 and 996. Perhaps, knowing all of that, Collin's announcement had been designed to generate publicity and keep the matter alive rather than to signal that a demonstration actually would occur. In any event, a few hours after the melee outside his headquarters, Collin announced that "pending a court decision" the NSPA would postpone its demonstration in Skokie, but that it would hold one "come hell or high water" before the year was out.

Frank Collin therefore was not in Skokie on July 4. The Jewish Defense League, however, was. About two thousand people looked on as thirty-one JDL members, primarily from New York City and Miami, marched in a parking lot next to the Jewish Community Center. They wore black motorcycle helmets and carried sticks and clubs. About a dozen of them also had on what the courts later described as "military fatigue-type clothing." Their "head of security" confided in reporters, "We hope the Nazis will come out so we can break their heads." Another JDL leader wearing a ski mask in spite of the summer heat worked the crowd. "What do we want?" the masked man yelled. "Nazis," the crowd replied. "How do we want them?" "Dead," came the reply. "Nazis dead. Nazis dead. Nazis dead." Kahane told the crowd through a bullhorn that when Hitler began his public career in a Munich beer hall, "There were Jewish lawyers like David Goldberger of the American Civil Liberties Union who said let them march." "Let us swear on this day that in a short time there will not be a Nazi office in Chicago," Kahane exhorted.

The parking lot was private property, and Skokie would later argue that the demonstration therefore was not covered by Ordinance 924. Goldberger noted that no other Skokie ordinances were interpreted as excepting private property unless the exception was made explicit by the statutes, which was not the case in the three new ordinances.

When David Goldberger and Gilbert Gordon appeared before the Illinois Appellate Court to argue *Skokie v. Collin* on the morning of July 8, the three judges indicated that they were inclined to give each side half a loaf.

"We consider the injunction [issued by Judge Wosik] to be illegal and ask that it be stayed," Goldberger told the court.

"There are special circumstances in this case," Gordon replied. "Here you have these Nazis wanting to wear uniforms with swastikas in Skokie, where there are 6000 residents who survived Nazi prison camps in World War II. By symbol, uniform and words, an appearance by the Nazis in Skokie would amount to assault on the survivors. Assault never has been protected by the Constitution." The "circulation of ideas in the marketplace so that people can make their own choice" was a good thing, Gordon went on. In this case, however, the court was confronted with people who "distribute pamphlets and material that promotes hatred." He did not believe they were protected by the First Amendment. "I don't think that a limitation on this kind of communication would have one whit to do with the lessening of democracy for persons with decent ideas."

Goldberger argued that it was not the government's function to define "decent ideas" and that the Constitution did protect symbolic speech, however obnoxious. "The issue is prior restraint," he told the court. "If you deny this communication because it is likely to be offensive, then you are allowing a hecklers' veto. If you have 200 hecklers following 30 Nazis around, you have a situation in which the majority decides who speaks. And then you have aborted the First Amendment; you have lost it." It was impossible to predict in advance what reaction the demonstration and its symbols would evoke, Goldberger said. But banning the swastika would in effect be a ruling that the government could ban any symbol it chose. The constitutional approach would be to permit the demonstration and arrest anyone who broke the law. The fighting words doctrine was not relevant because it was applied by the Supreme Court to situations in which, during a one-on-one confrontation, a person speaks words to another that are extremely likely to evoke a physical response before there is time for reflection.

Judge Thomas A. McGloon had a question for Goldberger. "Are you saying," he asked, "that it would be all right to wear a swastika into a synagogue?"

"No," the attorney replied. He rejected the implicit reference to the "captive audience" doctrine, which permits a broader exception to the right of free speech. While a synagogue congregation would be a captive audience, Goldberger said, there was nothing "captive" about anyone who chose to go to a demonstration.

Chief Judge Mayer Goldberg remained concerned about the symbolism of the swastika. Why, he asked, was it necessary for the NSPA to wear uniforms and swastikas in order to protest the three Skokie ordinances? The Constitution did not permit the government to decide what symbols could be used in protest, Goldberger answered. But the third judge, John M. O'Connor, joined his two colleagues in indicating that he too found the idea of Nazi speech in Skokie troubling, and court watchers speculated that the judges might hold that displaying the swastika there was not a right included in the First Amendment.

The court watchers were correct. On July 11, the court handed down a per curiam opinion permitting the demonstration but forbidding the display of the symbol.

The three judges clearly were smarting at the rebuke from the Supreme Court. They accused both sides of "grossly improper legal procedures" and castigated the ACLU for "some very grave procedural problems . . . lurking in the record." Equally unhappy with Judge Wosik, the court expressed puzzlement as to exactly what the injunction prohibited. "In the rush to judgment in this hastily briefed case," the judges scolded, a major issue had escaped notice. One part of the injunction seemed to them to enjoin the party from demonstrating in Skokie only if its members wore uniforms rather than civilian clothes, while both attorneys had framed their arguments as if the injunction banned any demonstration no matter what the demonstrators' apparel. The court, "rather than requesting further briefs and argument," treated the injunction as consisting of two parts, one enjoining a demonstration no matter what was worn and the second as prohibiting the wearing of the uniform.

Accepting Goldberger's argument that the demonstration was intended to be a peaceful assembly that included no "derogatory public statements directed at any ethnic or religious group," the court overturned the injunction to the extent that it prohibited the demonstration entirely. Such an injunction, the judges wrote, was a clear violation of the well-established legal doctrine that a potentially hostile audience could not be the basis for a prior restraint on the expression of ideas. That was not the case, however, with the uniform.

Citing *Tinker v. Des Moines* and *Cohen v. California*, the court agreed that "the wearing of distinctive clothing to express a thought or idea is generally the type of a symbolic act which is considered protected speech within the first amendment." But whether it was permissible speech under the circumstances depended on which part of the uniform was in question, which the court saw as consisting of two parts: the "storm trooper uniform" and the swastika. Wearing the uniform, the court held, was an expression of goals "similar to those of the German Nazi Party." The question for the court was whether expression of those goals was also "a direct incitation to immediate mass murder." Holding that there was not "one bit of evidence in the record that the uniform without the swastika would have such an effect," the court turned to the issue of the swastika. The record seemed to indicate that the uniform, "stripped of all other symbols," was unlikely to provoke a violent reaction and therefore came under the First Amendment's protection of symbolic speech. The court noted that "however odious and repulsive" the swastika was "to most members of our society," it was a symbol meant to communicate ideas. There was no showing that its display "will incite anyone to immediately commit mass murder" or "commit any unlawful act in furtherance of the goals of the defendant party." The judges were convinced that the display of the swastika in Skokie nonetheless fell into the category of fighting words.

Sol Goldstein had testified about the symbolism of the swastika and its possible effect upon him, the court noted, and Mayor Smith had said the people of Skokie felt it was a sight they could not and should not have to tolerate. The judges agreed. "The swastika is a personal affront to every member of the Jewish faith," they found, "inherently likely to provoke violent reaction . . . when intentionally brought in close proximity to their homes and places of worship." The affront was exacerbated for Holocaust survivors, said the court. That finding led the court to uphold the injunction on the display of the swastika during the course of any demonstration in Skokie. It differentiated the situation from the one addressed by the earlier New York case of *Rockwell v. Morris*, where the demonstration permitted by the courts was held in a large urban public park, not a "relatively small suburb of which persons of the Jewish faith constitute the majority." The court did not address the question of whether Skokie's Jewish "majority" would be affronted. That would have been difficult to establish, as the outrage of the Jews in Skokie was focused on possible harm to the survivors. Nor did the court indicate how an illegal "affront" was to be differentiated from one that was legal, other than by the possible reaction of the audience.

The court's use of the *Chaplinsky* fighting words doctrine was surprising because Skokie had not referred to it. It is usual for courts to decide constitutional issues by adhering rigorously to the arguments made by the two sides. Now, without argument on the point by the two parties, the court extended the fighting words doctrine substantially. It applied the fighting words doctrine to symbols, whereas the Supreme Court had used it only in reference to spoken words, and said that fighting words could be used in showing the need for prior restraint rather than merely in punishing it after the fact.

The judges ended their opinion by noting pointedly that the ruling did not negate prosecution of the defendants "should they incite violence" or prevent Skokie from enforcing the three ordinances, the validity of which was not before the court. They also assumed that the injunction was a temporary one, and their decision directed the trial court to hold an immediate hearing on the merits of one that was permanent. The order read that NSPA members "hereby are enjoined and restrained from engaging in any of the following actions within the village of Skokie until further order of the court: Intentionally displaying the swastika on or off their persons, in the course of a demonstration, march, or parade."

Collin promptly said he would not violate the injunction but would appeal further, and Goldberger began preparing papers to submit to the Illinois Supreme Court. Collin may well have been heartened when, on June 22, federal district court judge George N. Leighton issued a preliminary order in Collin's challenge to the Chicago Park District's insurance requirement.

A Seventh District Court of Appeals justice had written earlier that it might be reasonable for the city of Chicago to require that some form of indemnity be posted by prospective demonstrators, but as only private insurance companies could provide the commercial insurance needed to meet the bond requirement, the city had effectively and unconstitutionally turned the decision as to who could rally in the public parks over to private companies. Judge Leighton's decision explained why what seemed to be an eminently reasonable policy might violate the First Amendment. Asking demonstrators to ensure that a municipality will not be left holding any bill for damages is, on its face, a policy protective of taxpayers. But only groups wealthy enough to have general public liability coverage also have access to low- or no-cost special-events coverage of the kind required by the Chicago Park District. "It is particularly difficult for a prospective buyer to find such coverage," Judge Leighton wrote, "unless he has had previous business dealings with insurance companies or insurance brokers." When the insurance was available, it could cost up to $1,000 per event. Collin had testified that the party's usual end-of-month bank balance was approximately $250. Janice Irene Jarosz had told the court that the ACLU had asked her, a licensed insurance broker who worked for "a commercial line insurance agency specializing in the placement of business insurance," to obtain insurance for both the NSPA and the Martin Luther King, Jr. Coalition. She spent "at least thirty hours during the first six months of 1977" contacting thirteen insurance companies and brokerage houses. All of them refused to issue a policy to either group, and she was convinced there was absolutely no possibility of getting such insurance. There was no suggestion during the trial that she was mistaken.

"As the insurance requirement was so high that potential demonstrators could not cover it themselves," Judge Leighton ruled, it "effectively prohibits the plaintiff and the like . . . from applying for a permit . . . and restricts the exercise of First Amendment privileges." Groups that were new, small, or unpopular were at the mercy of private insurers, who could take into account "political beliefs and other invidious factors." The clear implication was that the requirement turned insurance companies into censors. Judge Leighton held that it was therefore "an unreasonable restraint upon First Amendment rights" as they might otherwise be exercised by "the ordinary person, organization or groups."

For the moment, it appeared that Collin was in sight of his original goal, which was to march in Chicago. He quickly applied for a permit to do so. The response of the park district was that Judge Leighton hadn't prohibited an insurance requirement; he had said only that $250,000 was too high an amount. The district told Collin that he would have to post bond for $60,000. Furious, Goldberger went back to Judge Leighton. The park district then said that there had been a misunderstanding: the date for which

Collin had applied was unavailable, but he could reapply for another one. Then, however, the district discovered that Collin's organization was not registered with the Illinois secretary of state and therefore failed to qualify for a permit. The outraged Goldberger asked Judge Leighton for a contempt order against city park district officials, and the judge took the motion under advisement. At the same time, Goldberger and Harvey Schwartz filed their respective papers with the Illinois Supreme Court. Goldberger asked the state's highest court to overturn the appellate court's injunction on the swastika; Schwartz, to overturn the decision giving the NSPA the right to demonstrate in Skokie. Repeating the pleas they had made in the appellate court, the two men argued the case before the supreme court in September 1977.

CHAPTER 6

The Price of Battle

The ACLU is very busy, but never too busy to stick up for the First Amendment.

NORMAN DORSEN, ACLU PRESIDENT

By September 1977, David Goldberger and the rest of the Illinois ACLU staff were reeling from the public response to the case. ACLU president Norman Dorsen sent Goldberger a book with a complimentary inscription. Thanking Dorsen, Goldberger wrote on September 23,

> The entire affiliate is feeling embattled and words of encouragement have been all too infrequent. . . . What started out as a distasteful but otherwise routine civil liberties case turned into an incredible battle. In Chicago the reaction of those to whom we normally turn for support has become increasingly hysterical.

So much of the national press was writing about Skokie and interviewing survivors there that it was hard for journalists to find new faces for their stories. Many of them turned their attention instead to what Goldberger called "the growing flood of criticism and outright verbal abuse" and to the increasing number of resignations by ACLU members.

The ACLU lost about thirty thousand members—15 percent of those who had belonged. The income that disappeared with them amounted to some $500,000 a year. While national executive director Aryeh Neier had warned in late 1974 that the organization was in financial trouble, he was unable to rectify the situation. As the Skokie cases worked their way through the courts and case expenses mounted, the national board ordered the staff to cut $200,000 in expenditures and stop publication of the *Civil Liberties Review*. The Illinois ACLU estimated that it had lost 30 percent of its anticipated income for 1977, and it laid off five of its thirteen employees.

ACLU affiliates around the country were dependent on the 70 percent of each member's dues the national office sent to them, and the escalating wave of resignations endangered the existence of many of the small Midwest and southern branches. Ira Glasser, who would replace Neier as the organization's executive director in mid-1978, headed the New York affiliate during Skokie. His December 1977 fund-raising letter described the situation there as "threaten[ing] to cripple the ACLU" and told New York members, "*All our programs are in jeopardy . . .* the contribution you usually make at this time of the year is particularly important." Glasser went on to explain why the ACLU brought suit against the Skokie ordinances:

> It is the same kind of law that was used in Birmingham, Alabama and throughout the South to stop civil rights demonstrators. . . . Of course there is a vast moral difference between the Nazis' speech in Skokie and Martin Luther King's demonstrations in the South. What we must all decide, however, is . . . whether it is in our best interests—yours and mine—for the ACLU to have entered the Skokie case in order to strike down the anti-demonstration law.

"We defend the First Amendment for everybody because there is no other way to defend it for ourselves," Glasser continued. What was at stake in Skokie was "not only the rights of those particular marchers in that particular place but the viability of the First Amendment and the rights of the rest of us."

ACLU leaders were trying everything they could think of to stem the flow of members. In August 1977, the national office solicited the signatures of sixty "prominent Jewish business and professional persons" on a press release. Among them were Abraham Brussell, former judge for the Circuit Court of Cook County; Monroe Friedman, former dean of Hofstra Law School; Ruth Bader Ginsburg, professor of law at Columbia University (and later a justice of the Supreme Court); journalists Daniel Schorr and Nat Hentoff; author Studs Terkel; Martin J. Oberman, a Chicago alderman; and two past presidents of the Chicago Council of Lawyers. They expressed their loathing for the Nazis but argued that the ACLU understood the "paramount importance of preserving the rights of free expression" and praised its stand in Skokie for being based on the recognition that "the rights of individuals are inextricably tied to the rights of all."

If the press release and other efforts had any effect on the membership, they were not discernible. Norman Dorsen, a renowned constitutional attorney and scholar as well as the ACLU president, later commented that the membership loss should have been anticipated. While it undoubtedly reflected disagreement with the ACLU's defense of the NSPA, he thought, it was at least as much a function of the ACLU's sudden and enormous growth in the 1970s coupled with a disorganized membership department incapable of keeping track of all the new people. Either the department or the firm sending out ACLU's mailings lost the files of about 20 percent of the members and could not mail renewal notices to them. Barbara O'Toole, too, thought the membership drop unsurprising. "We are equal opportunity offenders," she said of the ACLU. "I think we've offended everyone over the years."

The organization had grown dramatically in the 1970s. Many of its new members joined after September 1973, when the ACLU became the first national organization to call for the impeachment of President Richard Nixon; these memberships were probably a reflection of support for that action, rather than of any commitment to civil liberties. It was unheard-of for the ACLU to sign up fifty thousand people in a year, but that was what happened in 1973. Those who sent in their dues only because of the proposed impeachment, Dorsen believed, would have fallen by the wayside sooner or later; Skokie simply became the immediate cause of their doing so. David G. Barnum and Richard D. Bingham, two political scientists who studied the matter after the Skokie affair ended, came to the same conclusion. At the time, however, the ACLU felt itself to be under siege.

The organization was somewhat bewildered at what it viewed as the public's lack of comprehension. ACLU principles were clear, the organization's leaders thought; the principle behind its stand on free speech was the simplest of all. A month after Ira Glasser's letter explaining the ACLU's position on Skokie went out to New York members, the affiliate defended the right of the Jewish Defense League to picket in front of the Soviet mission on behalf of Soviet Jews. To the New York affiliate, that decision was as easy to make as the decision in Skokie had been to the Illinois affiliate. The ACLU also defended JDL members' right to picket the home and to attend a deportation of an alleged Nazi war criminal and represented Jewish demonstrators picketing Secretary of State Henry Kissinger in Baltimore for allegedly counseling U.S. actions favorable to Arab countries. The right to free speech was indivisible. Philosopher Carl Cohen, who had both chaired the Michigan affiliate and served on the national board of directors, wrote in the April 15, 1978, edition of *The Nation,* "Public offensiveness . . . is an unavoidable cost of freedom. . . . Exceptions cannot be made for nasty opinions. If the swastika is too offensive for some to tolerate today, the Star of David will be claimed equally intolerable by others tomorrow."

Many ACLUers, however, disagreed, believing that Skokie constituted a special case or that the ACLU should not spend scarce resources on a Nazi party. On March 20, 1978, the *New York Times* carried a letter from economics professor Abba P. Lerner. If the ACLU's purpose of promoting and defending "a democratic social order in which freedom of speech is secure . . . comes into conflict with freedom of speech directed at destroying such a democratic social order," he wrote, the organization's obligation was "to protect the social order of free speech rather than the free speech of its destroyers." Lerner argued that it was not "the *unpopularity* of Nazism that deprives Nazis of free speech rights," but rather "their opposition to that right for all, and their intention to destroy it." Their stand on free speech for others, Lerner felt, made it "monstrously impertinent" for them to claim it for themselves and a "grievous mistake" for the ACLU to represent them.

Aryeh Neier's response for the ACLU was published on March 27, 1978. Lerner's approach had been misused in the past, Neier said. "Senator Joe McCarthy and his colleagues who made decisions to deny freedom of speech to enemies of freedom did a clumsy job. They went after Stalinist Communists and anti-Stalinist Communists, people they regarded as fellow travelers and liberals they mistakenly identified as Communists." "Now, as in the McCarthy days," he cautioned, "freedom of speech can only be defended by resisting every incursion on the right to speak. The only social order in which freedom of speech is secure is one in which it is secure for everyone."

In April 1978, Neier went to Brooklyn Law School for a debate about Skokie. His opponent was from the National Lawyers' Guild, one of the organizations opposed to the ACLU's position on the grounds that civil libertarians should support only "progressive" groups. The debate was scheduled for April 20—Hitler's birthday. Neier himself had been born in Berlin on April 22, 1937. His mother had hinted that she held off delivering him as long as possible to avoid having his birthday coincide with the celebrations for Hitler. Although Neier and his parents escaped from Germany in 1939, three of his grandparents and several other relatives died in the Holocaust.

At the law school, Neier continued to spell out the ACLU position:

The right to free speech is always tested at the extremes. Rarely are centrist groups denied their First Amendment rights. It is almost always fringe groups—people who are provocative, who select that place where they are disliked the most because that is where they can get the most attention. Isn't that what Martin Luther King did at Selma? For that very reason it is the extremes that have the greatest interest in protecting the right of their enemies.

Once the freedom of one group is abridged, that infringement will be cited to deny the rights of others. The people who most need the ACLU to defend the rights of the Klan are the blacks. The people who most need the ACLU to defend the rights of Nazis are the Jews.

Given his early years, Neier's faith in the ACLU's position was breathtaking. He sent a letter to dissenting members in August 1977 and said in it, "One comment that often appears in letters I receive is that, if the Nazis come to power, the ACLU and its leaders would not be allowed to survive. Of course, that is true." One source of his commitment to civil liberties was, perhaps, mirrored in his next sentence: "Civil liberties is the antithesis of Nazism." Referring to pre-Hitler Germany, Neier noted,

The Weimar Republic had a law against group defamation. Typically, it was never invoked against Nazis. . . . To anyone familiar with the [Weimar] period, the notion that it died of an excess of civil liberty is the wildest nonsense. On the contrary, the Weimar Republic was incapable of protecting civil liberty. . . . Free speech did not exist in Weimar Germany because the government would not safeguard it.

He spelled out the reasoning behind his, and the ACLU's, stance:

We will only deserve to call ourselves a civil liberties organization so long as we continue to insist that everyone is entitled to freedom of speech. . . . The Nazis may despise us—and we certainly despise them— but we intend to continue to be governed by our rules and the rules of the United States Constitution. That means defending free speech for those we despise and those who despise us. It means not being governed by the rules of the Nazis. Their rules and the values they represent have already come to power if governments are allowed to pick and choose who is entitled to freedom of speech.

Norman Dorsen agreed. Responding to an article by Jim Mann in the *New Republic* that suggested the ACLU had better things to do than defend Nazis, Dorsen wrote in part,

The ACLU is very busy, but never too busy to stick up for the First Amendment. Mann ignores an ACLU operating principle: the ACLU takes *all* cases where our help is sought in protecting the freedom to speak; we take all other civil liberties cases selectively. . . . The ACLU remains, as always, dedicated first and foremost to the First Amendment.

Despairing ACLU leaders wondered why the rest of the world seemed not to understand the obvious. But the ACLU's position in Skokie was not at all obvious, or right, to others. When Neier got back to ACLU headquarters from his Brooklyn Law School debate, he was greeted by members of the Jewish Defense League, who handed him a brass plaque. It was engraved with the words, "Presented to the A.C.L.U. on Hitler's Birthday. Our graves are flooded with blood and tears. Our graves are crowded with the bones of our babies and families. Where are you, our brother?" The plaque was affixed to a large board bearing pictures of the concentration camp ovens in which Jews and others died. The entire display was covered with broken glass and simulated blood.

———

The ACLU position was not the obvious one to major American Jewish organizations, either. Before Skokie, the ACLU had often made common cause with the organized Jewish community on many issues, including that of speech. But, as the Anti-Defamation League's rejection of its own quarantine policy suggested, Jewish organizations found the Skokie case extremely difficult. Skokie became an instance of a clash of interest groups as well as a major case in American law.

———

Alexis de Tocqueville noted when he visited the United States in the 1820s that what he called "political associations" played a unique role in the public life of the country. Organized around the interests of their members and devoted to seeing their interests reflected in public policy, voluntary groups reflected the "eye of mistrust and anxiety" with which citizens viewed the government and their belief that they had to rely upon their "own exertions" if they were "to resist the evils and the difficult ties of life." He considered political associations to be a "necessary guarantee against the tyranny of the majority."

There were relatively few Jewish Americans when Tocqueville traveled through the United States. There was a vocal Catholic community, however, and he wrote about its members, "They constitute a minority, and all rights must be respected in order to ensure to them the free exercise of their own privileges."

In keeping with Tocqueville's thinking, the ACLU has become a major participant in the effort to negate the "tyranny of the majority" by safeguarding the rights of individuals. As one of its slogans indicates, it considers itself to be the country's "guardian of liberty." It came into existence not only because its founders wanted to guard the rights of the minority but because the founders saw themselves as constituting a minority, initially in their desire to question American involvement in World War I and then to safeguard the freedom of speech of others. Its history also includes so many instances of its fighting lonely battles for liberty that it could well view itself in 1977 as a constantly beleaguered expert on what liberty is all about.

To the ACLU of the late 1970s, free speech was the most important hallmark of liberty because of its role in a democracy. Freedom of religion was not far behind, however; and in order to protect it, the ACLU coalesced frequently with the organized Jewish community. Skokie became a testing ground for the alliance between major Jewish organizations and the most potent of the groups in the civil liberties community. As such, Skokie was also a harbinger of the decline of the working consensus that had been built up among proponents of individual liberty and those who supported governmental guarantees of equality. A societal awareness and validation of "roots" and the historical experiences of specific peoples such as Jews, African Americans, Latinos, Asian Americans, and Native Americans would have the unintended side effect of pitting the liberties of individuals against the rights of groups. Skokie was a glimpse of the future.

Of all the large Jewish organizations, the American Jewish Congress (AJC) was perhaps both the most civil liberties–minded. It was founded in 1916 with the active involvement of Louis Dembitz Brandeis, shortly to become a Supreme Court justice and one of the creators of the country's unique speech jurisprudence. The American Jewish Committee, created ten years earlier, occasionally joined ACLU efforts for religious freedom; but the American Jewish Congress was the Jewish group most often relied upon by the ACLU to support its positions. Brandeis's impassioned defense of the First Amendment was not unusual in the Jewish community, and certainly a disproportionate number of the ACLU's members were Jewish.

Estimates ranged from 20 to 40 percent. Jews constitute less than 3 percent of the population of the United States; and minority groups here are well aware, as Aryeh Neier wrote after Skokie, that they are most vulnerable to having their speech cut off. Tocqueville's recognition that it was natural for members of a small and relatively powerless religious community to emphasize their rights was equally true of American Jews in the twentieth century, particularly after the Holocaust.

As the Skokie situation developed, however, the question arose of whether the overlapping Jewish and civil liberties communities would find themselves at odds. This was all the more so after the Anti-Defamation League decided to sponsor the survivors' menticide suit. The AJC found itself sharply divided.

The AJC staff advised it in June 1977 that organizational policy had been to oppose injunctions against communication and that it should stay out of the Skokie dispute. A seemingly different position was taken by Naomi Levine, the lawyer who was the AJC's executive director, in August 1977. Levine sent a letter then to the Public Broadcasting Service's local outlet in New York City, where the AJC had its headquarters. She commended the station for deciding not to air a debate that featured Collin and David Duke of the Ku Klux Klan and denied that the decision constituted censorship. AJC staff lawyer Nathan Dershowitz, on the other hand, adopted the ACLU position. His September memo to Levine, written after the ADL and the American Jewish Committee had decided to support Sol Goldstein's menticide case, said, "I have very serious reservations about supporting this kind of Complaint and find it difficult to distinguish this situation from a legal point of view from the activities of civil rights activists and Vietnam protesters in the past."

When the AJC's Commission on Law, Social Action and Urban Affairs debated the matter the following month, it defeated motions to abstain entirely from the three cases, to file a brief supporting the appellate court decision enjoining only the wearing of the swastika, and to file a brief in that case opposing restrictions on speech—an indication both of the very differing positions the AJC was considering and of the extent of disagreements within it. Among the commission members were Alan Dershowitz, Nathan Dershowitz's brother; constitutional law scholars Norman Redlich, Alan R. Westin, and Abraham S. Goldstein; and economist Robert Lekachman. I. Martin Wekselman, a judge in Pittsburgh who had to miss the commission meeting, had written to the others,

I need not tell you that I yield to no one in my detestation of the American Nazis and their position; nevertheless, the guarantees of the First Amendment are so important to all of us that any attempted trimming of First Amendment rights, even in so extreme a case as that presented by the American Nazi Party, is in my view a serious mistake. We should do everything in our power to attempt to explain to the community in general, and to the Jewish community in particular, that a balancing of the interests involved simply requires that we support the position of free expression, even of those views which we find despicable.

ACLU leaders held a number of conversations with the ADL, the AJC, and the American Jewish Committee in late 1977 and early 1978. The conversations' failure was made clear in mid-January, when the AJC's national governing council adopted a statement declaring,

While the First Amendment guarantees free speech and expression, the courts have consistently made clear that free speech is not absolute at all times and under all circumstances. The U.S. Supreme Court has repeatedly stated that there are certain well-defined and narrowly limited classes of speech, the prevention and punishment of which on balance are not constitutionally protected. These include insulting or fighting words. . . .

Within this framework, we believe that the courts may and should prohibit the National Socialist Party of America (the Nazi Party) from marching through Skokie, Illinois, a community whose population consists of a very large proportion of Holocaust survivors and victims, if they display swastikas or uniforms which identify them as implementing the evil objectives of Hitlerism. . . . [A march without swastikas or uniforms] would not infringe on the right of the Nazis. It would not prohibit them from marching or parading in the City of Skokie. It would merely prohibit them from marching with swastikas or uniform [sic] which are an abusive, insulting affront to every Jews and particularly to that section of the Skokie population who are concentration camp survivors.

If the case was appealed to the Supreme Court, the press release continued, the AJC would file an amicus curiae brief taking that position. Such a brief is submitted by an individual or group not directly involved in a case but anxious to give a court information or a viewpoint that it might otherwise not have. The governing council's position was endorsed by the membership at the AJC's national convention in March.

Later that month, AJC national vice president Theodore Mann addressed the National Jewish Community Relations Advisory Council, a coordinating body for 9 Jewish agencies and 103 Jewish communities across the country that he chaired. His comments suggested the difficulty of the Skokie situation for organization leaders. "At war in Jewish hearts are two parts of our heritage—on the one hand, a profound commitment to the principle of unfettered freedom of expression, and, on the other hand, an anguished collective memory of the Holocaust," Mann said. After reaffirming the Jewish community's commitment to free speech, he spoke of the Holocaust as "a powerful molder of Jewish attitudes":

It is already becoming part of our liturgy, the traditional way of incorporating historical experience into the mind set of the Jewish people. I am gratified and terrified in about equal measure when I hear young Jews say that the Holocaust is the single most critical event that has affected their lives, even though it occurred long before they were born.

Mann said that the authors of the Constitution also knew about the "corrupting influence of power and that its invariable victim is individual freedom." They were well aware of the same "potential for evil" in human beings that the Holocaust made a permanent part of the Jewish consciousness.

The founding fathers of this nation were not pollyannas. Their realistic view of human nature, its potentiality for evil, man's lust for power, permeates the entire Constitution. They constructed a system of government [to prevent] overwhelming power . . . they believed that the majority would tyrannize the minority, and hence they adopted the First Amendment.

As the Constitution's authors recognized,

[m]an has been given the choice between good and evil and many, perhaps most, have chosen mostly the good. Those of us who will never forget the Holocaust, however, know that many have made the other choice.

Mann discussed the threat of anti-Semitism:

We are of course very sensitive to it and abhor it. But none of us would suggest the use of law to stifle it. What we are talking about now is not merely anti-Semitism. It is no less than the advocacy of our deaths— ours and our children and other loved ones—flaunted in the faces of those who already once in their lifetimes have witnessed the deaths of their children and other loved ones.

What the survivors were "crying out to all of us" was, he said, "Don't let this become the kind of society in which we must choose between supine betrayal of the memory of our loved ones on the one hand and violence on the other. Give us an alternative."

For Mann, as for the other leaders of AJC, the proposed "march" in Skokie differed from the "scores, perhaps hundreds of Nazi incidents" in the United States in the preceding fifteen years. The difference lay "in the magnitude of [the march's] potential for anguish and therefore violence." But he was still troubled by his conclusion, and warned against drawing a general principle from it. Skokie was different.

The AJC was far from the only Jewish organization divided by the Skokie situation. In September, Rabbi Balfour Brickner, director of interreligious affairs of the Union of American Hebrew Congregations, published an article entitled "Can We Tolerate Nazis?" in his organization's magazine. In it, he acknowledged the "psychological aggression" implicit in the proposed demonstration but argued that the country would be best served by maintaining a stance against government censorship. The article generated so much criticism that Brickner wrote to ACLU leaders, pleading for additional answers to give his critics. Milton Ellerin's November 1977 report for the Trends Analysis Division, Domestic Affairs Department of the American Jewish Committee was based on a survey of American Nazi groups such as the NSPA that he had undertaken for the committee. It found that "naturalized Americans who survived the holocaust understandably overrate the danger" in the Nazi clubs, which were riven by "discord, hatreds and petty jealousies" and had a combined membership of no more than 1,500 to 2,000. The report concluded, "Nazism in America is impotent." The committee decided nonetheless to oppose the demonstration in Skokie. In February 1978 Neier found it necessary to send a Jewish foundation in Massachusetts a seven-page report summarizing instances between 1941 and 1976 in which the ACLU had worked jointly with Jewish organizations to defend civil liberties, usually against violations of free speech, religious liberty, or racial equality.

———

The majority of the country's national media outlets, and almost all those based in Chicago, expressed understanding of the ACLU's position. The *New York Times, Washington Post, Los Angeles Times, Chicago Daily News,* and

Chicago Sun-Times were among the newspapers supporting its stand, which also was praised by CBS Morning News. The *Chicago Tribune* said on June 18, 1978, in an editorial entitled "On Rights and Nazis,"

> It is asking a great deal of them [the survivors] to counsel self-control in the face of the provocation like this. . . . The "National Socialist Party of America" and the sorry bunch of exhibitionists who belong to it are not the issue. By the nature of things, 1st [*sic*] Amendment battles often involve the rights of thoroughly disreputable people.

The editorial board added, on July 6, "More people should learn that the best weapon against extremist exhibitionism is a protracted yawn."

Rabbi Harold P. Smith, vice-president of the Hebrew Theological College, replied on July 15 that "if the writer of that editorial had seen his mother, fathers, brothers, and sisters—or possibly even his children—tortured and thrust into a gas oven as a manifestation of what the Nazi emblem and Nazi military uniform stood for and still stand for, he would (I hope) hardly have yawned."

Chicago columnists heaped scorn on Collin but counseled against turning him into a martyr. Jeff Lynn of the *Tribune* mocked him as "an Al Capp character named Frank Collin, who combs his hair and his mind to the side like Adolf Hitler." Collin was "the kind of guy," Lyon said, "who used to eat erasers in class and roll his eyeballs up into his head to get attention." (Lyon was equally contemptuous of Collin's opponents, mocking the "Communists and Socialists and Worker Laborites and Labor Socialists and other who just enjoy dressing up like Woodie [*sic*] Guthrie.")

Letters to the editors around the nation indicated that readers were torn. The outpouring in the Chicago newspapers was particularly intense. One reader wrote in April 1977,

> The clowns are coming to Skokie. We must greet them with the kind of parade and celebration that traditionally accompanied the arrival of a circus. . . . Let us fill Dempster Avenue with thousands of Jews celebrating the joy of their peoplehood. . . . It requires tremendous moral courage not to serve a knuckle sandwich on rye to a flaming idiot who is praising Himmler and calling for your extinction. Nonetheless, it is exactly those 1st Amendment rights of speech, assembly, and religion that allow us as Jews to pray as we feel, cultivate our unique heritage, educate our children in Jewish tradition.

"What gives Skokie authority to pass quickie ordinances that deny constitutionally guaranteed rights of free speech and assembly?" another writer demanded. On June 24, reminding readers of Collin's Jewish roots, columnist Mike Royko suggested what he thought was the best tactic: "For those who decide to take a peek at Collin, I have a suggestion. As he marches by, give him a big horse laugh and say: 'And so's your old man, Frank; so's your old man.'" (Royko added that the action of the Nazi Party in ejecting Collin from its ranks when it learned his father was Jewish struck him as fair: "If you are going to be anti-Semitic, you shouldn't play favorites.") Mrs. Desmond Hadhazy wrote a letter to the editor supporting the quarantine policy because "It hurts more to be ignored then [sic] opposed." A month earlier reporter Bob Wiedrich had written in a *Chicago Tribune* column entitled "Nazis deserved a cold shoulder" that Skokie residents "should have let the stumblebums march—alone" instead of giving Collin and "his flaky friends" the publicity they sought. "Free speech is the birthright of all Americans," Wiedrich added. "That includes the right to act like a jackass."

But those voices were drowned out by those of other readers. Elliot N. Schubert called the ACLU "myopic and naive" and charged that the "obvious intent of the Nazis is to provoke an incident between the marchers and the residents of Skokie," putting the Jews "in a bad light" and "provid[ing] the Nazis with a forum." Michael J. Tuchman argued that "allowing this group to demonstrate in support of genocide, especially in the communities of their intended victims, violates a principle that transcends any constitution." Three Christian students at North Park Theological Seminary wrote, "It would be a hate march against the Jewish people." Maidi Pritchard admonished, "A big yawn does not work; history has shown that. It was tried on Hitler. . . . Hitler, a society reject if there ever was one, came to power in a climate ripe for demagoguery. . . . We do not live in normal, stable times. . . . How do we know we are immune to contagion?" John Coebele expressed the sentiments of many others when he wrote, "Whatever 'reason' the Nazi idiots may have for wanting to march in Skokie . . . they would not be exercising free speech, but would be engaged in psychological war. They would simply be inflicting further anguish on people who have already suffered too much." Harry Bernard agreed: "It is not a 'peaceable' activity for Nazis or members of the Ku Klux Klan to march up and down a community in which many Jews or blacks are residents."

As 1977 drew to a close, the hemorrhage of ACLU members and criticism of David Goldberger continued. Harvey Schwartz, too, had taken beatings, although far fewer of them. Schwartz was well aware of the dismay his less-than-absolute First Amendment position had caused many of his fellow attorneys. He and Gordon recognized that they had not been able to articulate a line differentiating acceptable and unacceptable speech. Schwartz, who remembered "prominent Jewish judges" in Chicago telling him that his argument was "nonsensical," acknowledged ruefully that David Goldberger knew more about free speech doctrine than he did. When the two lawyers argued *Skokie v. NSPA* before the Illinois Supreme Court, Schwartz felt besieged. One of the justices, he recalled, "tore into me" for what the judge saw as Schwartz's cavalier attitude toward the First Amendment; the memory still rankled twenty years later. By the time of his appearance before the court, he had "become emotionally involved in the case and was pleading hard, talking about some of the things I had observed and what the survivors and their relatives had been going through." "I was just a lawyer" not used to arguing constitutional issues, he said. "I was just doing my job as a lawyer." But as he tried to get the court to understand the survivors' pain and the impact he believed it should have on the outcome of the case, one of the judges commented, "That has no place here. This ground has been covered before and you're not saying anything that is new." Schwartz was appalled:

I couldn't imagine that someone didn't grab out, didn't think about it— turn it into something even if I couldn't. . . . In my mind, Skokie at this time, with these sensitized people, was an exception [to the latitude that should be given to speech]. But nothing—just nothing.

For the most part, however, Schwartz did feel supported by his communities in both Skokie and Chicago, where he earned his living in private practice downtown on La Salle Street. Although he remembered that in the Skokie case "we were always battling uphill against the traditional concepts of First Amendment protection—prior restraint, all of those things," he also recalled that

[w]e were not only picking up political support, moral support, financial support; I mean internationally; but we were getting some legal minds going as well. We were never short of ideas. I couldn't walk down La Salle Street from my office to the courthouse without some

usually Jewish lawyer coming up to say, "Have you thought about this? or tried that?"

Money and letters of support poured in from all over the nation. When Schwartz and Mayor Smith visited Israel, Jerusalem's mayor, Teddy Kollek, gave Smith a medal; Kollek and Schwartz struck up a friendship.

As Schwartz was discovering, handling a highly publicized case has its share of both peaks and valleys. Losing a highly publicized case can be the deepest of the valleys. As the calendar crept toward January 1978, both Schwartz and Goldberger were waiting anxiously for the Illinois Supreme Court to hand down its opinion. In the meantime, however, they had a date in federal court.

CHAPTER 7

Verbal Cacophony

Slurs and insults which rely upon the victim's racial and religious heritage
are among the most vicious and abusive epithets known.
JUDGE BERNARD DECKER, *Collin v. Smith*

On December 2, 1977, Schwartz and Gordon, Goldberger and O'Toole were in Judge Bernard Decker's courtroom in federal district court. The case of *Frank Collin, et al. v. Albert Smith, et al.* was about to be argued.

Goldberger called Collin to the stand. Queried about his motives in asking Skokie for a permit, Collin replied that he wanted

> to conduct a public demonstration on the first of May in front of the Village Hall with approximately thirty to fifty uniformed members of our organization in paramilitary uniforms, with the swastika, as a part of our uniforms and on our placards, and the signs were to read "For Free White Speech," "Free Speech for White People," and the purpose of the demonstration was to protest the Park District's ban, as it were, against our right to free speech in that town.

Emphasizing what he insisted was the peaceful nature of his acts, he told the court that "our intentions always were to abide by the law until such time as we were able to demonstrate." He had said repeatedly that he would not to go Skokie until the ordinances were stricken and demonstrating was legal.

Schwartz asked him on cross-examination about the beliefs of the NSPA. "We believe that the Negro race is biologically inferior to the white Aryan race," Collin replied. "We believe, with the first five presidents of the United States, that the Negroes should be repatriated to their African homeland, as quickly as possible."

Gilbert Gordon wrote later that Skokie rested its case in *Collin v. Smith* entirely on the great psychological harm that the demonstration would do to the survivors and not at all on its original assertion about the hostility of the audience. Apparently Skokie's experience in the Illinois appellate courts had convinced its attorneys that the potentially-violent-audience argument could not be employed successfully. In order to lay the ground for the claim of harm, Schwartz introduced one of the Nazis' pamphlets into evidence while Collin was testifying. The lawyer told the court,

> This is a publication entitled "We Are Coming," with the swastika at the top, indicating the intention of the National Socialist Party of America to go into suburbs of Chicago, particularly Skokie, under a maxim which says: "Where one finds the most Jews there also one finds the most Jew haters." . . . [A]nd on the back page of it, your Honor, is a figure with a hand clutched at its throat with the words "Smash the Jew System."

Sol Goldstein added harrowing details about his experiences in Kovno. He remembered the day the Nazis separated the ghetto residents into two groups:

> Then came the S.A. Their leader was Mr. Jodl, with a yellow uniform, with a swastika. He reviewed the whole thing and started to segregate, "You go to the left. You go to the right. You go to the left, you go to the right," without telling the real reason why it is to the left and why it is to the right. . . . [At one point] I was between the 15,000, without knowing whether this was better or worse.

Harvey Schwartz asked Goldstein to describe the uniform worn by the NSPA.

> A: Very briefly, it is the same uniform as the S.A. in Nazi Germany.
> Q: What does that uniform and swastika mean to you?
> A: Death in a most terrible form; not only death to be shot in a moment to be killed but death after torture.

David Goldberger, attempting to show that the survivors sometimes sought out the sight of swastikas, asked Goldstein whether he considered himself typical of the survivor community.

> A: I am a survivor; what makes me typical?
> My history is not the most tragic. I was not in Dachau or Auschwitz, I was not a member of the Sonder Kommando who were ordered to burn the dead bodies.

Goldberger had Goldstein talk about seeking out some of Collin's demonstrations "downtown and on the South Side" and asked,

Q: Mr. Goldstein, you also testified as to what the uniform and the swastika mean. Do you own any books that have pictures of uniforms and swastikas in them at home?

A: Yes.

Goldberger replied to the psychological-harm argument by placing into evidence a map showing the downtown area around the village hall to be commercially zoned. All of the demonstration, he said, would take place within that area—not within sight of the survivors' homes. Goldstein had testified that his house was "a mile and a half north and a mile and a half, approximately, east" of the village hall. Goldberger's point was that any survivor who preferred not to see the Nazis was under no compulsion to do so. Skokie said that there were residential neighborhoods abutting the village hall area and that the front of the village hall could be seen from some. Although there was in fact at least one apartment building within viewing distance, no evidence was offered that any survivors or other Jewish residents lived there.

Police Chief Chamberlain was called to the stand and testified about the meeting Mayor Smith had held in his office in March 1977 to discuss the "annoying phone calls Mr. Goldstein was receiving." He repeated that they were "the highest volume of this type of call that we have ever received." Collin denied that he or his party was involved, and no village official suggested at the trial that the NSPA had made the calls. The officer who had taken a report from Goldstein said he doubted the NSPA was responsible—testimony that shored up Collin's insistence that he and the other NSPA members had acted within the law.

In order to show that the village was unconstitutionally singling out the NSPA for negative action, Goldberger went into the history of the enforcement of the ordinances. He referred specifically to the July 4 demonstration by the JDL on the Jewish Community Center's parking lot, in military-style uniforms, and to Skokie's tacit decision not to interfere with it because it was on private property. This is where Goldberger made his argument that no other Skokie ordinances were interpreted as excepting "private property" unless they specifically said so. Under questioning, village manager John Matzer was forced to concede that there were no written standards governing any waiver of the ordinances or cosponsorship by the village.

Donald Perille, chairman of the Skokie Plan Commission, spoke about the history of racism in Skokie to indicate that it was reasonable for the village to worry about violence. The testimony of the witnesses as a whole replicated that given in Judge Wosik's court; the legal arguments made by the attorneys paralleled those before the appellate court and Illinois Supreme Court.

Four days later the attorneys gathered once again to take the deposition of Dr. Gutmann in *Collin v. Smith.* Judge Carey had heard Goldberger's and Torshen's arguments in *Goldstein v. Collin* in August. He agreed with Goldberger that the plaintiffs were attempting to stop an activity clearly protected by the First and Fourteenth Amendments and dismissed the complaint. Goldstein was appealing that decision, however, so the two sides were seeking additional ammunition as they prepared for their presentations before the Illinois Supreme Court.

Those presentations were never made.

The Illinois Supreme Court handed down its decision in *Skokie v. NSPA* on January 27, 1978, lifting what remained of the injunction prohibiting the party from demonstrating in Skokie. Once again, the opinion was per curiam, and it represented the views of six of the seven judges who heard the case. The seventh, Justice William G. Clark, dissented without an opinion.

The opinion for the court stated that decisions of the United States Supreme Court, and particularly its holding in *Cohen v. California,* left the Illinois court with no choice: "[In] our opinion," they "compel us to permit the demonstration as proposed, including display of the swastika." Implicitly rejecting the appellate court's separation of symbolic speech from verbal speech, the court wrote that as "it is entirely clear that the wearing of distinctive clothing can be symbolic expression of a thought or philosophy," the "symbolic expression of thought falls within the free speech clause of the first amendment." The burden of justifying any imposition upon it rested with Skokie. The court turned to Skokie's invocation of *Chaplinsky* and the fighting words doctrine.

The *Chaplinsky* case was not a useful precedent, said the court, because it was clear that the Supreme Court's restatement of the fighting words doctrine in *Cohen v. California* was meant to be definitive. The Supreme Court had described fighting words there as "those personally abusive epithets which, when addressed to the ordinary citizen, are, as a matter of common knowledge, inherently likely to provoke violent reaction." Was display of the swastika such an epithet? The court thought not.

In *Cohen*, the Supreme Court had addressed the problem of reconciling what some might consider uncivilized speech with the right to speak. Recognizing that the right implied that "the air may at times seem filled with verbal cacophony," Justice John Marshall Harlan had nonetheless asked on what basis the government could possibly distinguish between a word that was offensive and one that was not. "Indeed, we think it is largely because governmental officials cannot make principled distinctions in this area that the Constitution leaves matters of taste and style so largely to the individual," Harlan wrote, adding that "one man's vulgarity is another's lyric."

Display of the swastika was "as offensive to the principles of a free nation as the memories it recalls," the Illinois court added, but it was nevertheless "symbolic political speech intended to convey to the public the beliefs of those who display it." If it was thrust upon a captive audience in an intolerable manner it might possibly be actionable. But

here, there has been advance notice by the demonstrators of their plans so that they have become, as the complaint alleges, "common knowledge" and those to whom sight of the swastika banner or uniforms would be offensive are forewarned and need not view them. A speaker who gives prior notice of his message has not compelled a confrontation with those who voluntarily listen.

The court cited the words of Justice Louis Powell in *Erznoznik v. City of Jacksonville* (1975), including Powell's quote from *Cohen v. California*:

[T]he Constitution does not permit government to decide which types of otherwise protected speech are sufficiently offensive to require protection for the unwilling listener or viewer. Rather, absent the narrow circumstances described above [home intrusion or captive audience], the burden normally falls upon the viewer to "avoid further bombardment of [his] sensibilities simply by averting [his] eyes."

The court "reluctantly" concluded that it was the "burden" of Skokie residents to "avoid the offensive symbol" if their reaction was likely to be violent.

Skokie v. NSPA was not the only Skokie-related case decided by the Illinois Supreme Court that day. It also agreed to hear the appeal in *Goldstein v. Collin* and immediately ruled in the case without having asked for written briefs or oral argument. The court agreed with Judge Carey that the proposed demonstration was a constitutionally protected activity and directed him to dismiss the case. In its one-paragraph summary order, the court added that there was no stated cause of action; Goldstein and the other survivors therefore lacked standing to sue; and as Goldstein was asking for the kind of injunctive relief already sued for by the village, the case was redundant. By stating that there was no cause of action, the court in effect rejected menticide as a valid legal concept. The United States Supreme Court would decline to hear Goldstein's appeal. Whether or not Collin could demonstrate in Skokie appeared to hinge on whatever Judge Decker decided.

He overturned the three Skokie ordinances on February 23, in a fifty-five-page decision that surveyed the history of free speech jurisprudence in the United States and might well serve as a minicourse about it.

Judge Decker had first to decide whether the NSPA had enough at stake to bring the suit. Suggesting that he could have declared the case to be moot (not a real conflict of interests), he noted that Ordinance 994 regulated only those public assemblies that could "reasonably be assumed to exceed 50." Collin had whittled his expected number of participants down to between thirty and fifty, so the ordinance technically might not apply to him. But "in light of the criminal penalties the ordinance imposes for lack of foresight," Decker said, "the court feels that plaintiffs are the best judge of their need for a permit," and so he ruled that the NSPA had standing to sue.

The first substantive question he framed was whether "the burdensome effect" of the insurance requirement was necessary. The answer was no because, while the government could impose "reasonable" fees for demonstration permits, there was no rationale for making the figure an arbitrary and overly burdensome $350,000. His second point was that the ordinance had been implemented in a "standardless manner," as some groups were allowed to demonstrate without meeting the insurance requirement but there were no written criteria for waivers of it or for cosponsorship by the village. Decker understood that Ordinance 995, prohibiting racial slurs, was enacted to shield the citizens of Skokie "and particularly its Jewish citizens—from the flaunting by plaintiffs of the symbols of a hated era and repugnant political philosophy." But the ordinances "do more than simply ban display of the swastika; they impose sweeping bans on the content of speech within Skokie and include provisions for which there is almost no precedent in constitutional law." That being the case, he considered it necessary to examine "the basic principles of the First Amendment against which these ordinances must be measured."

Decker turned to the Supreme Court's enunciation of the clear and present danger doctrine, mentioning that the Court had held in 1974 that "there is no such thing as a false idea" under the First Amendment *(Gertz v. Robert Welch, Inc.)*. He was well aware, however, that the notion of a marketplace of ideas had met with the criticism that "to permit an idea to be advocated is to concede its legitimacy and impliedly accept the possibility that it may be accepted and implemented as a social policy" and that it had been argued that "there are some policies whose implementation would be so completely unacceptable in a democratic society that their advocacy should not be permitted." If any philosophy could be regarded as "completely unacceptable to civilized society" it was the one espoused by the NSPA when it identified itself "with a regime whose record of brutality and barbarism is unmatched in modern history." Decker rejected the notion that there were no false ideas. He asserted that the correct interpretation of the theory behind the First Amendment was that false ideas did exist but that they had to be condemned by the marketplace and not by the government. Here Decker quoted from Justice Brandeis's concurrence in *Whitney v. California,* and added,

> The question, then, is not whether there are some ideas that are completely unacceptable in a civilized society. Rather the question is which danger is greater: the danger that allowing the government to punish "unacceptable" ideas will lead to suppression of ideas that are merely uncomfortable to those in power; or the danger that permitting free debate on such unacceptable ideas will encourage their acceptance rather than discouraging them by revealing their pernicious quality.

This was "one of the fundamental dilemmas of free speech," but it had been decided "definitively" by the Supreme Court and that decision was binding on the nation. Judge Decker cited *Brandenburg v. Ohio,* which established the doctrine that speech could be prohibited only when it was likely to incite imminent lawless action. Skokie had given up that argument, however, specifically stating in one of its briefs that it did not contend that hate speech would create a clear and present danger of violence.

Skokie had asserted that racial slurs were fighting words. Decker interpreted the *Cantwell, Chaplinsky,* and *Terminiello* cases as holding that in order to meet the standard for fighting words, speech had to be "abusive and insulting rather than a communication of ideas," no matter whether the ideas might offend some listeners. The decision in *Cohen v. California* exemplified that principle.

Some speech, such as fighting words, was nonetheless unprotected by the Constitution, and Decker acknowledged that "the line between protected and unprotected speech in matters relating to race and religion is an extraordinarily difficult one to draw." On the one hand, racial and religious slurs and insults "are among the most vicious and abusive epithets known." At the same time, "discussion of race and religion will often involve the exposition of ideas and position that are inherently offensive to many, but which are nevertheless protected by the First Amendment." He continued,

> For example, plaintiffs believe that busing school children in order to accomplish integration is a threat to the integrity and quality of the public school system, and they also believe that blacks and Jews are the instigators of busing. . . . [A]t what point does a vehement attempt to arouse public anger at busing become an attempt to incite hatred of blacks and Jews? A society which values "uninhibited, robust and wide-open" debate cannot permit criminal sanctions to turn upon so fine a distinction.

Ordinance 995 punished "dissemination" of material that incited hatred, including the distribution of leaflets and the wearing of symbolic clothing. The ordinance therefore was not aimed "solely at personally abusive, insulting behavior," but at the communication of ideas.

Judge Decker was mindful of the dangers of hateful speech:

> It may very well be true that hatred tends to spawn violence and that, unlike the unrest and dissatisfaction referred to in *Terminiello,* hatred serves no useful social function in itself. Nevertheless, the incitement of hatred is often a byproduct of vigorous debate on highly emotional subjects, and the basic message of *Cohen* is that a great deal of useless, offensive and even potentially harmful language must be tolerated as part of the "verbal cacophony" that accompanies uninhibited debate, not for its own sake, but because any attempt to excise it from the public discourse with the blunt instrument of criminal sanctions must inevitably have a dampening effect on the vigor of that discourse.

The next question was whether racial slurs fell into the category of words that "by their very utterance inflict injury." Referring to Dr. Gutmann's testimony that the mere presence of Nazis in Skokie would be harmful to the survivors, Decker characterized Gutmann's perspective as "colored by his own interpretation of free speech and by his strong opposition to plaintiffs' political views" and not grounds for a legal decision. "It is particularly difficult to distinguish a person who suffers actually [*sic*] psychological trauma from one who is only highly offended, and the [Supreme] Court has made it clear that speech may not be punished merely because it offends." Skokie's argument that group libel could legitimately be forbidden could not rest on Gutmann's views alone, and the village had also relied on the precedent of *Beauharnais v. Illinois*. While that case had "proven remarkably sterile as a source of constitutional law," Decker wrote, it had never been expressly overruled, so it was his obligation to determine "whether the *Beauharnais* statute itself would pass muster if it were brought before the Supreme Court today." Decker thought it would not. He said of the decision in *Times v. Sullivan*,

> The Court concluded that seditious libel prosecutions are *per se* unconstitutional, and further that the government may not presume that criticism of official government policies will automatically reflect on the personal reputations of the responsible public officials. There can be no question that races and religion have been and are the subject of legitimate debate, and the Court's reasoning casts considerable doubt on the propriety of presuming damage to individual members of a group from criticism of the group.

Judge Decker found Ordinance 994 to constitute a prior restraint on speech that did not overcome the presumption of unconstitutionality for three reasons. The first was that it posed a high risk of "freewheeling censorship"; the second, that by Skokie's own admission the speech prohibited by the statute as applied to Collin did not present a clear and present danger of violence. The final reason was that the absence of procedures for making decisions about granting a permit and for appealing negative decisions meant that "the permit system lacks adequate procedural safeguards."

Ordinance 996 was similarly invalid. The only reason offered in its preamble for disallowing "military-style uniforms" was that such apparel was "repugnant . . . to the tradition of civilian control of government" and to moral standards in Skokie. Those justifications, Decker said, were "patently insufficient." It was obvious that the ordinance was "directed specifically at Nazi uniforms and regalia" rather than at *any* military-style uniforms, because there was no indication that Skokie meant to prohibit things such as "an appearance by members of the American Legion in support of the candidates of the Democratic or Republican party." Decker wondered aloud whether passage of 996, so "patently and flagrantly unconstitutional on its face," reflected "bad faith harassment" on the part of the village.

At the end of his opinion, Decker reiterated his "acute aware[ness]" of the dangers inherent in public statements of racial and religious bigotry: "In this case, a small group of zealots, openly professing to be followers of Nazism, have succeeded in exacerbating the emotions of a large segment of the citizens of the Village of Skokie who are bitterly opposed to their views and revolted by the prospect of their public appearance." The appropriate legal response, he thought, was suggested by Justice Holmes's opinion in the case of *United States v. Schwimmer* (1929).

Dissenting from a decision that the government could deny a citizenship application because the applicant was a pacifist, Holmes wrote, "[I]f there is any principle of the Constitution that more imperatively calls for attachment than any other it is the principle of free thought—not free thought for those who agree with us but freedom for the thought that we hate."

Decker added a word of his own: "The ability of American society to tolerate the advocacy even of the hateful doctrines espoused by the plaintiffs without abandoning its commitment to freedom of speech and assembly is perhaps the best protection we have against the establishment of any Nazi-type regime in this country." In effect, he held that there is no right not to be insulted when the insult is part of the expression of ideas.

By examining the Supreme Court's free speech jurisprudence and ruling that *Beauharnais* was no longer operative law under it, Decker helped make that true. His opinion is one of the definitive statements about the theory and practice of speech under the American constitution.

————

At the end of the 1980s many college campuses introduced codes of permissible speech. The courts' rejection of the codes as violations of the First Amendment relied in good part on Judge Decker's decision in *Collin v. Smith*.

Racial intimidation and harassment had become a major problem on a majority of the nation's college and university campuses during the 1980s.

As more people of color and women of many races became students at all levels of higher education and were emboldened by their numbers to be more assertive about being treated in a nondiscriminatory manner, as the nation's economy contracted and people looked for a scapegoat, as the country realized that the problem of racism could be articulated but not cured by short-term phenomena such as the civil rights movement, the number of incidents increased. A fraternity at the University of Wisconsin-Madison, for example, decided in 1988 that the best way to raise funds would be to hold a "slave auction" in a private residence. Some of the young men pledging the fraternity donned blackface paint and Afro wigs for pejorative skits. In one, a pledge pretended to be Oprah Winfrey while two fraternity members took turns voicing sexual taunts. The university's chancellor withstood demands by two hundred students who took over the administration building for a "day of rage," insisting that the fraternity be put out of business and its "entertainers" expelled. The university did, however, enact a speech code.

At Stanford University in the fall of 1988, white and African-American students discussed composer Ludwig van Beethoven's ancestry. The African-American students said that Beethoven was a mulatto; the white students, that he was entirely white. When a poster of Beethoven was subsequently vandalized by two of the white students, who added stereotypically black features to his face and then hung the poster in a mostly black dorm, there was a nasty confrontation. Stanford responded by tightening its hate speech code.

That year an African-American student at Smith College found a message under her door reading, "African Nigger do you want some bananas? Go back to the Jungle." In 1989 a blackboard in a University of Michigan classroom bore a sign parodying advertisements placed by the United Negro College Fund: "A mind is a terrible thing to waste—especially on a nigger."

Unfortunately, one could recount hundreds of similarly racist, sexist, anti-Semitic, and homophobic incidents on campuses in the years between 1985 and 1990. The atmosphere created for students from the groups stigmatized by such incidents, Stanford Law School's Professor Charles Lawrence wrote, amounted to one that denied equal educational opportunity. Being "forced to live and work in an environment where at any moment they may be subjected to denigrating verbal harassment and assault" necessarily affects students' ability to learn: "The testimony of nonwhite students about the detrimental effect of racial harassment on their academic performance and social integration in the college community is overwhelming."

Opponents of speech codes agreed with that assessment but doubted that limitations on speech would achieve anything other than driving hate speech and the attitudes behind it underground. The real answer to racist speech, they argued, lay in exploration of the unarticulated reasons for the prejudices expressed and education designed to alter racist attitudes. They also pointed to the difficulty of finding words that would eliminate "bad" behavior but permit "good" speech to flourish. The University of Pennsylvania code, forbidding "any behavior . . . that stigmatizes or victimizes," had been used to charge an undergraduate who called a group of women African-American students outside his dorm window "water buffalo." There was no objective way to measure the "stigmatization" or "victimization" caused by the epithet or to differentiate it from annoying or even offensive speech, civil libertarians asserted, and the First Amendment protects such speech. (The charges ultimately were dropped.) A federal court made this point about Michigan's code, noting that when applied to a student's classroom comment that homosexuality was a disease, it clearly penalized "offensive" rather than illegal speech and that the speech in question could not have been punished off the campus. Haverford College's code acknowledged that "precise criteria for identifying discrimination or harassment are hard to establish."

Courts in Wisconsin, Michigan, and Connecticut struck down the speech codes of their respective state universities as violations of the First Amendment. Judges referred to the Skokie cases as indicating that even heinous speech came under the amendment's protection and that constitutional laws specifically aimed at eliminating particular forms of speech probably could not be written. After the United States Supreme Court overturned a local Minnesota law criminalizing symbolic speech (*R.A.V. v. St. Paul,* 1992), the speech code movement ran out of steam.

———

The only affected party who knew nothing of Frank Collin's victory in Judge Decker's court on February 23 was Collin himself. When the decision was handed down, Collin was somewhere between Chicago and St. Louis, battling a blizzard. The publicity-minded NSPA leader was therefore unable to take advantage of his moment of glory.

Collin went to St. Louis to help organize a "national convention" of the NSPA that he and Michael Allen, the head of the St. Louis branch, announced would bring out 150 members. The event took place on March 11 and, as reported by the media, was less than a success. The 40 or 50 neo-Nazis attending decided to march in their uniforms through the shopping district of an old south St. Louis German neighborhood called Gravois, where the NSPA had recently opened an office, and into Gravois Park. They left their headquarters under heavy police protection, described by *New York Times* reporter Douglass E. Kneeland as consisting of "a bus and two vans loaded with policemen, a motorcycle escort and foot patrolmen along the route." Aryeh Neier was told that 175 police officers were in protective attendance as the party members rode in a rented U-Haul flatbed truck draped with banners that read "Remember Rockwell" and "White Freedom." Looking out, its passengers saw what appeared to be a hostile crowd of thousands. They promptly decided not to descend from their vehicle, which took off for Gravois Park followed by a crowd of teenagers and twenty-somethings throwing snowballs and a few stones and bottles. The Nazis cowered behind their "White Power" signs.

Along the way, Collin and his companions learned that awaiting them in the park were several hundred counterdemonstrators led by the JDL and the Revolutionary Socialist League, most of them yelling, "Smash the Nazis!" They were also told that there seemed to be little support for them among the residents of the old neighborhood. Deciding not to hold their demonstration after all, and still protected by police, they retreated to their headquarters. The counterdemonstrators followed, and the building had to be secured by more than one hundred police officers clad in riot gear.

The little drama's last act was played out there. JDL national director Bonnie Pechter was one of the people waiting outside the building. Although she told reporters that her wig and large glasses signified that "I'm in disguise," she promptly removed them when television crews appeared. For their part, the Nazis decided that what they really wanted to do was go home, and the police agreed to their request that they be escorted to a district precinct house for safety. There they cowered inside for several hours until someone showed up with their civilian clothes. Giving up their plan to reassemble at headquarters, they quickly changed out of their uniforms and disappeared.

Collin, apparently disconcerted by the lack of popular support, said he was considering calling off the demonstration in Skokie that he had planned for April 20—Hitler's birthday. Michael Allen, the St. Louis NSPA leader, declared the demonstration a success. What part of it he was referring to was unclear.

When Collin got back to Chicago and found out about Judge Decker's ruling, he apparently regained his morale and jubilantly announced that he would demonstrate on April 20 after all. Realizing that was a Thursday rather than part of the weekend, however, he switched the date to Saturday, April 22—which was also the first day of the Jewish holiday of Passover.

Many of the survivors, anguished at the court decision and the real possibility that the demonstration now would take place, met on March 7 at the Janusz Korczak Lodge. Erna Gans told the press that they had agreed to hold a countermarch expected to involve fifty thousand people. The Public Affairs Committee of the Jewish Federation of Metropolitan Chicago, a committee in which Goldstein was heavily involved, said the next day that it would support the counterdemonstration. In addition, it would organize a week-long educational program on the Holocaust. On March 13 an article in the *Chicago Tribune* reported that at least fifteen Korczak Lodge members had received obscene or threatening phone calls early in the mornings following the survivors' announcement. Mayor Smith said that while there had been calls before, the number had reached "epidemic" proportions.

A Skokie resident reacted to Collin's announcement of the April 22 demonstration by taking out an advertisement in a local newspaper, advising the village to spread horse manure on the streets an hour before the demonstration. A town car dealer announced that he had served with General Patton during World War II and he was damned if he'd let the Nazis march. "There is an undercurrent of panic" in Skokie, a journalist reported. The JDL's national office contributed to the rising tensions by telling the press on March 14 that it wanted to see five thousand to seven thousand JDL people lining the streets of Skokie during the demonstration and that it was prepared to use violence to stop the "march." People from around the country began calling the American Jewish Congress to inquire about chartered flights to Skokie on the day of the demonstration. *St. Anthony's Messenger,* a Catholic weekly with a circulation of 280,000, published an editorial advising American Catholics to wear a yellow six-pointed Star of David on April 22 if the Nazis marched then. The Catholic War Veterans called the planned demonstration "odious, offensive and obscene" and joined the national Jewish War Veterans in condemning it. Illinois governor James R. Thompson expressed his support for the counterdemonstration and said he would join a protest some distance away from the Nazi band.

By March 16, thirty-four major Chicago Jewish organizations were working on the counterdemonstration and the Holocaust Remembrance Week scheduled to begin a month later. Several thousand people were expected at an open-air interfaith service, sponsored by the Niles Township Clergy Forum as a kickoff on March 19, in Skokie's Niles West High School stadium. Citing the increased tensions, Skokie asked Judge Decker to delay the effective date of his ruling until the Court of Appeals for the Seventh Circuit could hear the case. Schwartz told the court that between the NSPA rally and the counterdemonstrations being planned by "many different organizations representing tens of thousands of persons," there was "a threat to the well-being to the Village of Skokie, which is exacerbated by the absence of a final adjudication of this cause." On March 17 Judge Decker handed down a stay of the injunction for forty-five days, saying that it would "permit a cooling off period while this case is heard by the Seventh Circuit."

Goldberger, surprised that a federal court would allow a prior restraint on speech to continue, promptly petitioned Decker to end the stay. When the judge refused to do so, the attorney turned to the appeals court itself. On March 31 a three-judge panel rejected his contention that the stay was an unconstitutional prior restraint but scheduled the case itself for argument. Goldberger appealed to the Seventh Circuit Court of Appeals once again. There would be no demonstration until and unless it overturned the stay.

———

Back in early February, within days of the Illinois Supreme Court's rulings, David Goldberger taped a segment for the Phil Donahue television talk show and received a good deal of praise for it. That month the American Jewish Committee released its November 1977 report, "American Nazis—Myth or Menace," that said there were only 1,500 to 2,000 Nazis in the United States. They had a knack for getting media coverage but not for action. The AJC found that in spite of its paltry twenty-five to thirty uniformed members, the NSPA was nonetheless "among the best organized of the neo-Nazi movements in the United States"—raising the question of whether any of those movements could possibly be effective. *New York Times* journalist Douglas Kneeland would report in April that according to a new study by the Anti-Defamation League there were fewer than 1,000 Nazi "storm troopers" in the United States and that their organizations frequently were "at war" among themselves. The Skokie episode and NBC's showing of its series on the Holocaust, he wrote, "have brought the American Nazis a notoriety that seems to be greatly disproportionate to their numbers." The FBI told Kneeland it had "discounted the Nazis as a threat" and abandoned its surveillance of them several years earlier.

The fact that the Nazis posed no danger to the security of the United States did not negate the possible harm their presence in Skokie might do to some of the survivors. Some reactions to the Illinois Supreme Court decision reflected a continuing concern. On March 2 Representative Calvin Skinner of the Illinois legislature introduced two bills designed to keep the NSPA out of Skokie, saying as he did so that the measures might be struck down by the courts but would delay any march by three to five months. One denied a parade permit to any group in the state conspiring to violate any law or the civil rights of others. The second prohibited parades by any group promoting the use of physical force or "arous[ing] reasonable apprehensions" that it promoted the use of force. Among the acts it would outlaw was the display of symbols associated with "political violence." The two bills quickly gained support from other legislators.

Members of Congress also reacted to the court's actions. Orin Lehman of New York told the House of Representatives that "where there is reasonable assurance that Nazi or similar activity will be used to incite violence, it must not be allowed." A law banning such an activity would have to be very carefully crafted, Lehman admitted; and while he said he strongly opposed the planned "march," it was notable that he did not specifically say that it should be enjoined. Representative Abner Mikva of Illinois said in a press conference at his Skokie office that every legal avenue should be explored and that if there was a march, he would help plan a counterdemonstration "that will not only show what we as Americans oppose, but what we stand for." Frank Haiman of the ACLU, a friend of Mikva's and a former chair of the representative's academic advisory committee, replied publicly that he shared Mikva's "revulsion for everything represented" by the Nazis but thought the congressman wrong in thinking that there was any constitutional way of preventing a demonstration. The *Chicago Tribune* carried an article by Senator S. I. Hayakawa of California in which he urged that a demonstration not be allowed to take place. Senator Charles Percy of Illinois called for a counterrally and encouraged Skokie to continue legal action designed to negate the demonstration.

On the last day of March, a three-judge panel of the Seventh Circuit court denied Goldberger's request that it vacate Decker's stay order but set up an expedited schedule for disposing of the case. Skokie's brief was due on April 28 and the NSPA's on May 12; oral argument would be held during the week of May 22 or May 29. Responding either to the public turmoil or to other judges' disagreement with the panel's decision, the court announced on April 5 that the entire eight-judge court would reconsider it promptly. Oral argument on the merits was pushed forward to April 14.

Collin then sent Skokie another demonstration permit request. His April 11 letter said that the NSPA proposed to demonstrate on the sidewalk in front of the village hall from noon to 12:30 P.M. on Sunday, June 25. "The public assembly will consist of more than 50, but less than 100 demonstrators marching in single file, back and forth," he wrote, presumably using the fifty-or-more number to underscore his need for a permit. Covering all possible legal objections to his plans, he added, "The demonstrators do not anticipate the need to occupy the entire sidewalk and will adjust the line of march to accommodate normal pedestrian use of the sidewalk" and "No handbills will be distributed at the assembly . . . no speeches are planned." The letter asked for an alternative date if there were other potentially conflicting events scheduled for June 25. The village made the request public on April 15. A group of Skokie's Christian churches brought 2,500 Christian and Jewish residents together in a high school auditorium that day for a prayer service, handing out black armbands with yellow Stars of David. Simon Wiesenthal, the human-rights activist who in 1960 had tracked down Nazi war criminal Adolf Eichmann in Argentina, was at the Chicago Pick-Congress Hotel to receive the Jewish Decalogue Society of Lawyers' annual Merit Award. He told a press conference that he had a plan for dealing with the march, but would not reveal it.

Illinois state senator Howard W. Carroll introduced a bill modeled on the law upheld in *Beauharnais*. It and a measure sponsored by Senator John Nimrod paralleled the two proposed by Representative Skinner. Carroll's made the "public display of racial hatred" a misdemeanor and permitted anyone who would be affected by such a display to secure an injunction against it; Nimrod's prohibited parades that aroused "reasonable apprehensions" that they had been organized for the purpose of using physical force to promulgate beliefs. On May 2 the Senate Judiciary Committee unanimously endorsed the two bills and sent them to the senate floor for a full vote of the body. They were passed on May 10 by votes of 44–10 and 40–14.

While other branches of government worked at preventing the demonstration, the courts continued to hold that it would be legal. The Seventh Circuit appeals court handed down its decision on May 22, affirming Judge Decker's ruling that the ordinances were unconstitutional. "The result we have reached," said Judge Wilbur F. Pell Jr.'s opinion for the three-judge panel, "is dictated by the fundamental proposition that if these civil rights are to remain vital to all, they must protect not only those society deems acceptable, but also those whose ideas it quite justifiably rejects and despises." The court ordered Skokie to issue a permit for the June 25 demonstration. Mayor Smith responded with a promise to take the case to the Supreme Court.

The stage appeared to be set for a major confrontation. Some critics of First Amendment jurisprudence would soon argue that the case never should have been permitted to get that far. They identified themselves as Critical Race Theorists, and their critique is explored in the next pages.

CHAPTER 8

The Critics

*This was not an exchange of ideas. The presence of these symbols
was literally an assault.*

HARVEY SCHWARTZ, ON THE SURVIVORS'
REACTION TO THE SIGHT OF SWASTIKAS

"In addition to the harms of immediate emotional distress and infringement of dignity," legal scholar Richard Delgado has written, racial insults
cause long-term emotional harm and damage to their victims' career pros-
pects, social mobility, interracial contacts, relationships with those of their
own race, and physical well-being (black Americans, for example, are more
prone to high blood-pressure levels, stroke, and hypertension than white
Americans). Delgado's article "Words That Wound: A Tort Action for
Racial Insults, Epithets, and Name Calling," published in the 1982 *Harvard
Civil Rights-Civil Liberties Law Review,* became a "founding" text of the new
school of legal analysis known as Critical Race Theory. It was a call for
legal recognition of the damage that can result from hate speech and creation of a tort—a harm done by one person to another, which can be
grounds for a lawsuit in civil court—based in part on the existing tort of
intentional infliction of emotional distress. Referring to the Skokie situation as an example of the way they feel hate speech should *not* be handled,
Delgado and other Critical Race Theorists have criticized the traditional
civil libertarian approach to the law of speech in the United States.

So have many feminist theorists. And the practice of every other nation in the world that has codified its policy toward hate speech is in direct opposition to American speech jurisprudence. What is the substance
of these critiques, and what might be learned from them?

Critical Race Theory (CRT) was created by legal scholars in the late 1970s.
Recognizing that the civil rights movement of the 1950s and 1960s had passed
its peak, they were extremely concerned by the failure of the movement

to achieve racial justice in the United States. They saw the dominant institutions of American society as continuing to perpetuate racism in their daily practices even while those institutions professed to condemn it. In 1981, students at Harvard Law School, reacting to the departure of the African-American faculty member who taught "Race, Racism and American Law," demanded that the administration hire a person of color to teach it. The administration refused. Students then organized an alternative course, taught by faculty located elsewhere and by practicing attorneys of color, that was based in part on the thinking about racism and law that had been taking place on law school campuses since the late 1970s.

Critical Race Theorists such as law school professor Mari Matsuda consider the necessary guiding principle of law to be antisubordination: a prohibition on the law's giving anyone dominance over anyone else. They hold that the expression of views that, if adopted, would result in the societal subordination of specific groups is both distinguishable from the expression of other ideas and unacceptable. The difference they find in such speech is reflected in the alternative vocabulary they use. Racist speech thus is referred to as "assaultive speech," the implication being that such speech constitutes a punishable attack on individuals separately and in their collective identities. The first sentence of *Words That Wound: Critical Race Theory, Assaultive Speech, and the First Amendment,* a collection of articles by leading critical legal theorists, is "This is a book about assaultive speech, about words that are used as weapons to ambush, terrorize, wound, humiliate, and degrade."

Many feminist legal critics and Critical Race Theorists share a belief that the power of dominant political and economic forces in this society is utilized to keep disadvantaged groups subordinate and that the theory of rights is used to maintain and reinforce the status quo. They are skeptical about the liberal presumption that laws can be neutral, because such "neutrality" precludes differentiation among quite differing phenomena of very different social value. According to this argument, the right to free speech in the United States, which permits racists and sexists to utter racial slurs without fear of private legal action or punishment by the state, helps perpetuate racial and gender stereotypes. The continuing stereotyping buttresses racist and sexist practices, thereby depriving women and people of color of power, equality, and dignity. Because matters of race and gender are central to American politics, economics, social relations, and law, any legal rule that permits the expression of prejudice against historically mistreated groups necessarily harms not only those groups but the very idea of equality itself and prevents a potentially democratic society from becoming one that is truly just. Speech *is* action; the speech/action dichotomy used in speech jurisprudence is artificial and does not reflect reality.

Both critiques, then, reject the idea that law is neutral rather than an instrument through which the values implicit in it are translated into the possession of societal power. Their concern is for the distribution of power and the inequalities that currently lie in that distribution. Legal rules that sustain inequality are, by definition, unjust. Both groups argue that there must be a systematic recognition of differences if the society is to rid itself of the legacy of racism and sexism. The psychological context of speech is different, they aver, when slurs are directed at people of color and women. The history of discrimination, stigmatization, and societally imposed inferiority has left them vulnerable to "words that wound" in a way that is distinguishable from the hurt done to white Americans and men by group insults. At the same time, slurs against historically disadvantaged groups reinforce the very stereotypes and negative values that are relied upon to justify discrimination. A variation of the first argument was used to support the survivors' position in *Skokie*.

The women's movement of the 1970s initially relied upon the Fourteenth Amendment's equal protection clause, which prohibits governmental entities from denying anyone the equal treatment of the laws. Treat men and women the same way, feminists had thought, and the result would be equality of the sexes. The feminist legal critique, however, grew out of a reaction to the idea that equality could be achieved by no more than "sameness" of legal prescription.

Large parts of the feminist movement came to believe that *sameness* of treatment would not necessarily result in *equality* of treatment. Unless public policy recognizes differences as necessitating different treatment, the new argument went, some people inevitably would be treated unequally. An inability to recognize that fair health policies will take women's pregnancies into account, for example, results in such ludicrous phenomena as the Supreme Court's decision in *Geduldig v. Aiello* (1974). There the Court looked at a state government health insurance plan that covered voluntary sterilization procedures for men, accidents sustained as a result of sports activities, and elective cosmetic surgery, but not the cost of prenatal care and the birth of children in normal pregnancies. Its holding was that the plan did not violate the equal protection clause, because no one, no matter what his or her gender, was covered for pregnancy. (The reaction to *Geduldig* and a similar case involving a private company, *General Electric v. Gilbert* [1976], was passage of the federal Pregnancy Disability Act of 1978, mandating such coverage in otherwise inclusive benefits plans.)

Asserting that the legal system had to recognize differences, feminist legal critics began to wonder whether the expression of some *ideas* also ought to be treated in a different way when the expression constitutes the kind of assault on gender equality that many of them found in pornography. Their answer is implicit in the thinking of feminists such as Catharine MacKinnon, whose *Toward a Feminist Theory of the State* (1989) and *Only Words* (1993) argue that pornography is more than speech. MacKinnon sees pornography as an assault on the idea that women should be treated as subjects rather than objects and, by extension, on the possibility of gender equality. She refers to pornography as "women's Skokie." (It should be noted that other leading feminists oppose government censorship even of pornographic speech.) Similarly, Critical Race Theorists assert that racial epithets and insults are an assault on the principle that people of different races are of equal importance, and, thereby, on the possibility of our society's identifying and undoing the racial inequality that pervades it and its institutions and practices.

Many Critical Race Theorists hold that the only people who can make legitimate decisions about whether real harm is done by hate speech are the victims themselves. The question for critics of CRT therefore becomes whether Critical Race Theorists, in saying that there are no objective standards by which to decide what speech is harmful and how harmful it is, would make law too subjective and indeterminate. The concept of indeterminacy is drawn from Critical Legal Studies, another school of American jurisprudence, which holds that supposedly "neutral" American principles of law in general and rights theory in particular simply perpetuate existing inequality and injustice. Law embodies specific values and enhances the status quo, Critical Legal Studies scholars aver, and this is particularly evident in the area of speech. They accuse traditional American legal theories of embodying indeterminacy, or the absence of truly objective criteria for determining what is fair and just. The admission that all law is based on values and on particularistic definitions of good and bad is a prerequisite for the societal ability to understand exactly what the legal process is all about.

Critical Race Theory and Critical Feminist Legal Theory go one step further, seeing Critical Legal Studies as insufficiently illuminated by a recognition of the overriding importance of race and gender to American institutions and dynamics. All legal categories are not equal, they maintain, and merely suggesting that they are value laden is not enough. It is true, as Critical Legal Studies scholars allege, that society must not hide behind false "absolutes" but must identify and justify the values embodied in law. Society, however, must also focus attempts to articulate and legitimate public policies on the elimination of its two greatest injustices, which are inequalities based on race and gender.

The bottom line of CRT and the radical feminist legal critique, as they apply to speech, is that the formal collective arm of society—the government—must distinguish between speech that constitutes the valid presentation of ideas, on the one hand, and, on the other, speech that is in effect part of a pervasive societal pattern of subordination. The bottom line of the traditional civil liberties approach, by contrast, is the assumption that while individuals can and should condemn racist and sexist speech, the danger in having the government decide which speech is punishable is so great that it outweighs whatever benefits might flow from a formal communal condemnation of some speech. The two approaches to hate speech thus represent opposing opinions about the ability of the marketplace to differentiate between good and bad speech, as well as about the dangers or benefits that flow from giving the government a power to censor unacceptable ideas.

There is no reason, critical theorists assert, to assume that consumers in the marketplace of ideas will "purchase" the idea of equality, when all of American history shows the opposite to be true. The language of inequality becomes a tool employed to shore up the house of injustice. Civil libertarians reply that the critics' right to speak in this society, and to explore aloud ways in which speech wounds, is paradoxically the best answer to their critique. Speech that challenges existing concepts and institutions is most in need of the First Amendment's protection, because such speech is by definition the kind of speech that the society finds threatening. It is the speech that the majority, acting through the government, would be most likely to silence in the absence of a prohibition on government's entering the marketplace and declaring some goods unworthy of sale. Given that power, the government would deprive society of the kind of challenges to orthodoxy that have been embodied in the abolitionist movement, the labor movement, the civil rights movement, the women's movement, the gay- and lesbian-rights movement, and so on. The harm to individuals that can be done by speech is not as great as the harm that would continue to be done to them were society not able to engage in discussions about rights, justice, and equality. The terror that southerners felt at the call for Black Power, for example, could have been grounds for state governments to stifle speech in the 1960s had it not been for the theory of the First Amendment.

Critical theorists, whether their particular objection is to racist speech or to sexist speech, rely on the ability to differentiate. Some speech simply is different, they say, and the kind of decision making that society undertakes every day about what policies best apply to specific situations should be extended to the realm of communication. This is the kind of argument made by some observers of the Skokie matter.

Many of the letters that poured into the offices of the ACLU and of newspapers after the Illinois affiliate accepted the case expressed a belief in free speech as a norm that was irrelevant to the particular circumstances of Skokie. On June 29, 1977, the *Chicago Tribune* published a letter from Michael J. Tuchman saying, "Allowing this group to demonstrate in support of genocide, especially in the communities of their intended victims, violates a principle that transcends any constitution." John Coebele added, on July 25, "Whatever 'reason' the Nazi idiots may have for wanting to march in Skokie . . . they would not be exercising free speech, but would be engaged in psychological war. They would simply be inflicting further anguish on people who have already suffered too much." Harry Barnard wrote the following month, "It is not a 'peaceable' activity for Nazis or members of the Ku Klux Klan to march up and down a community in which many Jews or blacks are residents."

Abbot Rosen, head of the ADL's Midwest office, summed up the argument when he told journalist Nat Hentoff in August 1977,

Look, I am of the liberal left and I am a First Amendment person. When the Nazis demonstrate on Michigan Avenue, one of our main streets, I recognize their First Amendment rights—even though there may be Jews and even survivors of the Holocaust in the audience. But when the Nazis deliberately seek out a place—Skokie—where there are many

Jews, including survivors, then the question of intent becomes terribly important.

It is the difference between the Nazis marching in Greenwich, Connecticut, and marching in those parts of Rockland County where there are Hasidim [an orthodox Jewish sect], some of whom barely escaped the ovens [of the death camps]. The same act of demonstrating which is all right under the First Amendment in Greenwich becomes an intentional, specific assault against the Hasidim. I'll put it another way. In front of a Veterans Administration Hospital, as the paraplegics come out for recreation, a group of demonstrators, with signs and chanting, ferociously advocate euthanasia for paraplegics because they are too great an economic burden on society. Is that a legitimate exercise of free speech or is it an assault from which the paraplegics should have been protected?

One of the Illinois ACLU lawyers replied, "Do you know what this case comes down to? The people in Skokie think they have a constitutional right not to be insulted. There is no such right." Her position was that the right to hear includes the right not to hear, to shut out speech by not being available to hear it. Unless the situation involves a "captive audience," as in a school, any person who might be hurt or offended by speech can leave or stay away. This was all the truer in Skokie, where the entire community had advance warning of when and where the NSPA would express its ideas. The village's initial plan to "quarantine," ignore, the NSPA, was indicative of the many methods individuals or communities can employ other than quashing speech. To the Skokie survivors, however, absence was the equivalent of cowardice, of running away, of abdicating responsibility—but hearing the speech was too traumatic to bear.

When the entire series of events was over, some Skokie survivors told journalists of their dismay at not having been able to confront Collin and the others. In the face of a threatened Nazi demonstration, and with the knowledge of the horrific harms done by other Nazis, they would have welcomed a chance to talk back. And so they could have done, ACLU leaders indicated, by neither seeking an injunction nor supporting passage of the three ordinances, but by mounting a large and peaceful counterdemonstration. In the Holmes and Brandeis formula, good speech could have been used to counter bad speech.

Both the ACLU and its critics were seemingly discussing the Skokie situation when in fact it was the larger context that was of greatest concern to both. Those who opposed the demonstration did so against the background of the Holocaust and of events that had occurred thousands of miles away. Those who argued for a strict interpretation of the First Amendment did so not because of any sympathy for the NSPA but because of concern about the effect of the outcome on free speech doctrine all over the United States. The ACLU could not withdraw unless someone showed how the doctrine of permitting government to outlaw some speech could be kept from destroying the expression of the very ideas that might aid the cause of equality and justice. Skokie could not end its opposition because of the unusual sympathy and sense of community evoked by the survivors. It was, as David Goldberger said in Judge Wosik's court, a classic First Amendment dispute.

CHAPTER 9

The View from Abroad

*[Any publication or document] is undesirable [if it] is blasphemous or is offensive to
the religious convictions or feelings of any section of the inhabitants of the Republic;
brings any section of the inhabitants of the Republic into ridicule or contempt;
is harmful to the relations between any sections of the inhabitants of the Republic.*

PUBLICATIONS ACT OF 1974, SOUTH AFRICA

The major difference between a classic speech dispute as resolved by the
United States and one that occurs elsewhere in the world lies in the rela-
tive weight given to the individual's rights and responsibilities. While
a sharp distrust of government and a concomitant emphasis on rights
emerged from the American historical experience, most other nations
emphasize rights as being exercised within the context of obligation to the
community.

This certainly is true of the nations of Europe. The European Convention for the Protection of Human Rights and Fundamental Freedoms of
1950, for example, was signed by countries such as Austria, Belgium,
Cyprus, Denmark, France, Germany, Greece, Iceland, Ireland, Italy,
Norway, Spain, Sweden, Turkey, and the United Kingdom—and by the
United States, as such documents can be signed onto by nations in other
areas of the world. Article 10 declares that "everyone has the right to . . .
freedom to hold opinions and to receive and impart information and ideas
without interference by public authority and regardless of frontiers." The
next clause, however, introduces a note that makes the Convention quite
different from the Constitution of the United States:

> The exercise of these freedoms, since it carries with it duties and re-
> sponsibilities, may be subject to such formalities, conditions, restrictions
> or penalties as are prescribed by law and are necessary in a democratic
> society, in the interests of national security, territorial integrity or public
> safety, for the prevention of disorder or crime, for the protection of
> health or morals, *for the protection of the reputation or rights of others,* for
> preventing the disclosure of information received in confidence, or for

{ 123 }

maintaining the authority and impartiality of the judiciary. (emphasis added)

Article II, which addresses the right of peaceful assembly, forbids restrictions on it unless they "are necessary in a democratic society . . . for the protection of the rights and freedoms of others." The idea that rights are balanced by responsibilities has been present in the laws of some European nations at least since the late eighteenth century and the Declaration of the Rights of Man and the Citizen, adopted by France at the time of the Revolution of 1789 and still in force today: "The unrestrained communication of thoughts and opinions, being one of the most precious rights of man, every citizen may speak, write, and publish freely, provided he be responsible for any abuse of this liberty in those cases determined by law."

The clearest statement of the right to speech and the responsibility of exercising it with consideration for others may be in Germany's Basic Law of 1949, as amended in 1994. The first operative clause of the document declares that "the dignity of man is inviolable." Article 2 observes, "Everybody has the right to self fulfillment in so far as they do not violate the rights of others or offend against the constitutional order or morality." In keeping with that avowal, the article dealing with speech has two relevant sections. The first proclaims that "everybody" has the right to communicate and that "there shall be no censorship." The second adds, "These rights [of expression and reporting] are subject to limitations embodied in the provisions of general legislation . . . and the citizen's right to personal respect." Germany's Constitutional Court has interpreted the Basic Law to mean that human dignity is its highest legal value and that the state is obligated under the law to create a climate in which human rights can be exercised.

It is not only countries in Europe that focus on the nexus between rights and responsibilities rather than on rights alone. The 1969 American Convention on Human Rights, signed by the United States, declares, "Every person has responsibilities to his family, his community, and mankind," and goes on to say, "The rights of each person are limited by the rights of others, by the security of all, and by the just demands of the general welfare, in a democratic society."

The balancing of individual rights and the obligations of each person to the community is particularly evident in other nations' policies toward group libel. Argentina, Australia, Brazil, Cameroon, Chile, China, Colombia, Cuba, France, Germany, Great Britain, Mexico, Netherlands, Niger, Senegal, Spain, Sweden, and Venezuela are among the countries that criminalize racist speech. The laws of the Czech Republic, Denmark, France, Iraq, Israel, Jordan, Madagascar, Mauritius, Panama, Portugal, Spain, Sudan, Sweden, and Syria prohibit defamation of religious groups. French law has prohibited incitement to hatred against ethnic, national, racial, or religious groups or gender since 1972. In 1990 France enacted a statute making denial of the Nazi genocide of Jews a criminal offense. The German Criminal Code outlaws attacks on "the human dignity of others" that are likely to breach the peace because of "inciting to hatred against part of the population" or "insulting, maliciously making them contemptible, or defaming them." Denmark's Penal Code provides up to two years' imprisonment for anyone who publicly "makes a statement . . . by which a group of people are threatened, insulted or degraded on account of their race, colour, national or ethnic origin or religion."

Similarly, the 1973 revision of India's Penal Code makes it illegal to promote, through speech or pictures, "disharmony or feelings of enmity, hatred or ill-will between different religious, racial, language or regional groups" or to suggest that "members of any religious, racial, language or regional group or caste or community" cannot be good citizens or should be deprived of their rights as citizens. Words that "cause or are likely to cause . . . disharmony or feelings of enmity or hatred or ill-will between such members and other persons" are similarly proscribed. Argentina makes "anyone who in whatever way encourages or incites to persecution or hatred of a person or group of persons of a particular religion, ethnic origin or colour for reasons of their race, religion, nationality or political views" subject to punishment. Uruguay adopted a 1989 law threatening imprisonment for between three and eighteen months to anyone who "publicly or by any means suitable for dissemination incites any person to hatred or contempt . . . against one or more persons by reason of the colour of their skin, their race, religion, or national or ethnic origin." Namibia's Racial Discrimination Prohibition Act of 1991 and New Zealand's Race Relations Act of 1971 are among the many national statutes that criminalize incitement to racial disharmony. The 1986 amendment to Israel's Penal Law defines racism as "persecution, humiliation, vilification, the display of enmity, hostility, or violence, or the causing of animosity towards a community or parts of the population, all by reason of color or racial affiliation or national-ethnic origin" and makes racial incitement punishable by imprisonment for three to five years. Canada criminalizes "inciting hated against any identifiable group where such incitement is likely to lead to a breach of the peace" or "willfully promote hatred against any identifiable group."

The theme is to be found in many international human rights conventions, such as the 1965 International Convention on the Elimination of All Forms of Racial Discrimination. It condemns all "ideas or theories of superiority of one race or group of persons of one colour or ethnic origin, or which attempt to justify or promote racial hatred and discrimination in any form" and calls upon nations that have signed the convention to criminalize all dissemination of such ideas, provision of any assistance to racist activities, and organizations that promote and incite racial discrimination. The International Covenant on Civil and Political Rights, adopted by the United Nations in 1966, states that "the individual, having duties to other individuals and to the community to which he belongs, is under a responsibility to strive for the promotion and observance of the rights recognized in the present Covenant." Article 19, concerning freedom of expression, says that the exercise of the right "carries with it special duties and responsibilities," including "respect of the rights or reputations of others." The covenant also calls for "any advocacy of national, racial or religious hatred that constitutes incitement to discrimination, hostility or violence" to be prohibited by law. The United States has signed the convention, as have over a hundred other countries, ranging alphabetically from Afghanistan to Zimbabwe. (In signing the covenant, the United States declared that it did not read it as requiring action that would restrict the rights of free speech and association as they are found in the Constitution and laws of the country.) In 1981 the United Nations' General Assembly adopted a Declaration on the Elimination of All Forms of Intolerance and of Discrimination Based on Religion or Belief, to which the United States is a party. The African Charter on Human and Peoples' Rights adopted that year proclaims the rights to receive information and express opinions, within the context of maintaining "relations aimed at promoting, safeguarding and reinforcing mutual respect and tolerance."

Scholar Donald P. Kommers, analyzing German and American speech jurisprudence, has commented that "the purpose of political discourse in German theory is to create a tradition of civility and a polity of responsible citizens." He differentiates this from the tradition in the United States, which he finds best described by Justice Robert Jackson. In a case brought by Jehovah's Witnesses against a state requirement that students recite the pledge of allegiance even if their religion prohibited them from doing so (*West Virginia v. Barnette*, 1943), Jackson wrote, "If there is any fixed star in our constitutional constellation, it is that no official, high or petty, can prescribe what shall be orthodox in politics, nationalism, religion, or other matters of opinion or force citizens to confess by word or act their faith therein."

Some of the difference between American speech jurisprudence and that of much of the rest of the world can be explained by the different historical eras in which each developed. The First Amendment, along with the rest of the Bill of Rights, was adopted in 1791. As indicated earlier, it reflected a fear of centralized power and was worded so as to limit the activities of the new national government rather than of the states. The United States can take credit for its eighteenth-century enunciation of a doctrine of human rights, or civil liberties. The lack of any subsequent debate in the United States about the rational limits of speech and the way in which protection of individual rights is dependent upon the existence of a viable community has served the country less well. Absent the Brandeisian idea that speech not only is a matter of individual self-fulfillment but also is crucial to a democratic society and that each citizen has a positive obligation to answer what he or she considers to be bad speech with good speech, the current imbalance between commonly accepted rights and assumed but unarticulated responsibilities will remain uncorrected. The lacuna may lie less in theory than in discourse. We have a philosophy of citizen responsibility but we rarely articulate it; when we do, it can be too easily confused with an attack on the theory of rights. Communitarians such as Amitai Etzioni and Michael J. Sandel chastise civil libertarians for what they view as an overemphasis on individual rights and a selfish ignoring of the needs of a cohesive community. Their frustration can be understood as a result of the failure of American political discourse to articulate the seamless connections between the individual and the society.

There is little meaning to rights unless they are recognized and protected. The existence of a community is central to the practical acknowledgment of rights. Each individual therefore has a stake in the continuation of a vibrant community and, having such an interest, must assume the responsibility of taking an active part in it. In the area of speech, this means that the right to speak and hear carries with it the burden of listening, thinking, joining the ongoing debate about matters of interest to the society, and speaking with civility. The last does not imply failing to state one's beliefs even if the expression of them may hurt the feelings of others. It does, however, suggest that there are limits to what should be said, where, and how, if the fabric of a community is not to be torn. Whether those lines of demarcation ought to be taught by the community as each citizen's necessary restriction on herself or himself or whether society should accept the dangers of authorizing governmentally defined limits on speech, and what the potential dangers and benefits of each approach might be, is what the debate is all about. It underlay the two clashing viewpoints found in Skokie.

Another major issue has to do with the efficacy or lack thereof of hate speech laws.

Whatever international conventions they have or have not signed, most of the world's nations view speech as a right at least theoretically inherent in human beings and basic to democracies. The Universal Declaration of Human Rights declares that "the advent of a world in which human beings shall enjoy freedom of speech and belief and freedom from fear and want has been proclaimed as the highest aspiration of the common people." The first session of the United Nations General Assembly in 1946 adopted a resolution saying, "Freedom of information is a fundamental human right and . . . the touchstone of all of the freedoms to which the United Nations is consecrated." As the various nations' constitutions and basic laws indicate, the only acceptable reason for limitations on speech is the prevention of serious harm, whether the harm is to the state (breach of peace, endangerment of national security) or to the individual (the psychological harms caused by hate speech). The argument for abridgment of speech is tied to the efficacy of abridgment: it is valid only if it achieves a substantial societal value. The laws of many nations indicate that abridgment of speech is permissible only when there is no other way in which to avoid the harms potentially done by it. This means that if hate speech laws don't work, there is no legitimate reason for their existence in a democratic society.

Great Britain and the United States have legal systems that are rooted in similar if not identical doctrines and values. Early American law was based largely upon English law, although the two systems have followed different paths since then. Britain now has had some years of experience with hate speech laws and can be examined for an indication of their effectiveness.

The Public Order Act enacted in 1986 modified already existing English law designed to minimize hate speech. In voting for it, some members of Parliament referred to the law as a reaction against the fear, alarm, and distress that had been caused to members of minority groups and as an attempt to deal with the racial discrimination that might be linked to racist speech. They were concerned about the damage done by hate speech to the reputations of target groups and about possible consequent economic damage, such as loss of business and loss of employment.

The act punishes persons uttering threatening, abusive, or insulting speech with the intention of stirring up hatred against a racial group. Existing laws already criminalized racist speech with direct effects on public order. The 1986 statute gives police officers the power to exercise prior restraint over public assemblies, including deciding their location, the number of people who can be present, and the amount of time allowed. The power can be employed by a senior officer of police if he or she has a reasonable belief that one of the three evils specified in the act may result or that the assembly's organizers intend to intimidate a target group. The three evils are public disorder, serious damage to property, and serious disruption to the life of the community. Any assembly of twenty or more people is subject to the limitation if it takes place in a public space that is "open or partially open to the air" or a private space other than a home, on the theory that those with racist views may be further incited to racial hatred and public disorder by hearing hate speech.

Oddly, the statute as written would seem to permit racist speech among any number of people as long as it takes place within a residence, but not racist speech exchanged by two friends strolling along a street. Leaving that aside for the moment, the law states that speech can be punished if it is "threatening, abusive or insulting." The question of what constitutes abuse or insult is not addressed by it, nor is the dilemma of what is to happen if one person feels insulted but another does not. Some commentators have wondered whether Shakespeare's *Merchant of Venice,* with its negative depiction of Jews, could be banned under the law. Speech can be punished if the speaker *intends* to stir up hatred against a racial group, whether or not such hatred is *likely* to be stirred up. Assessment of intent is a factor in many areas of the law, but it seems particularly difficult to differentiate careless and potentially hurtful but real discussions of issues of race, or religion or gender, from speech intended to hurt.

Some of the impetus for laws against hate speech in Britain in the 1970s came from Jewish students on university campuses who were concerned about anti-Semitic speech. They and other students persuaded the National Union of Students to adopt a 1974 regulation against speech on campuses by "racist and fascist organizations." After the United Nations General Assembly passed a 1975 resolution equating Zionism with racism, however, the regulation was used to keep Zionist speakers—including the Israeli ambassador to Great Britain—off campuses. Among the first people prosecuted under the British Race Relations Act of 1965 were Black Power leaders. It is doubtful that the proponents of the National Union of Students' regulation or of the Race Relations Act intended either of those effects. In fact, the National Union of Students, disgusted with the results of its resolution, repealed it in 1977.

Canada is another nation whose legal system resembles that of the United States. The Canadian Supreme Court adopted a statutory definition of pornography that originally was part of a law proposed by Andrea Dworkin and Catharine MacKinnon (who referred to pornography as "our Skokie") for the city of Minneapolis. It embodied the idea that pornography violates women's civil rights and defined its production, sale, exhibition, or distribution as discrimination against women. Passed by the Minneapolis city council in 1984 but vetoed by the mayor, the ordinance was somewhat revised and then enacted by the city of Indianapolis. (It was invalidated by federal courts as a violation of the First Amendment.) The first prosecution under the Canadian version, which allowed the government to prosecute sexually explicit expression it believed to be "degrading" or "dehumanizing" to women, was against a gay and lesbian bookstore and the lesbian magazine it carried. Canadian authorities also used the law to prosecute bell hooks, the American black feminist author, and seize 1,500 copies of her *Black Looks: Race and Representation*. Ironically enough, Canadian customs officials, relying on the Supreme Court decision, confiscated two of Andrea Dworkin's books that bookstores were attempting to import from the United States. They did not, however, find sexually explicit art in *Penthouse* magazine to fall under the act.

The lesson is that hate speech laws are as discretionary as any other laws: they may be used against people whose speech we like or those whose speech we hate, depending upon who is in power and making the decision about which forms of speech fall under the laws. It is rarely the speech of the powerful that is banned by such laws. When the University of Michigan speech code was adopted, it was heralded as a blow against bigotry, but not a single white student who used racist language was held to account under it. White students used it about twenty times to charge black students, however, and one black student was punished for using the term "white trash." (The speech code was struck down by a federal court in 1989.) In discussing the issue of enforcement, African-American civil libertarian Henry Louis Gates Jr. tells of an exchange of epithets between a white police officer in Louisiana and the mother of a black suspect.

Police officer: Get your black ass in the goddamned car.
Mother: You god damn mother fucking police—I am going to [the Superintendent of Police] about this.

Only the mother, who later denied having used any profanity, was prosecuted for using "fighting words" (*Lewis v. City of New Orleans*, 1974).

The logical answer to the question raised by these examples of selective enforcement might seem to be a call for fairer enforcement. Civil libertarians would reply that ideas are so dangerous in their ability to convince that the people against whom speech is spoken are those most likely to find the speech threatening to society, morality, and so on.

Perhaps the greatest question about the efficacy of hate speech laws in combating racial discrimination is raised by the laws of South Africa during the decades when it practiced racial apartheid. Incitement to racial hostility was first banned in South Africa in the Black Administration Act of 1927 (revised in 1978). A series of acts and administrative regulations enacted through 1987 reinforced the prohibition on hate speech. The Publications and Entertainments Act of 1963, for example, banned all documents that the Publications Control Board deemed "undesirable." Included among these were publications "harmful to relations between sections of the inhabitants of the Republic." The Publications Act of 1974 expanded on the definition of "undesirable" documents and included any document that "brings any section of the inhabitants of the Republic into ridicule or contempt" or "is harmful to the relations between any sections of the inhabitants of the Republic." The Publications Act defined a "section of the population" as "a substantial number of people who as a result of an inherent characteristic or characteristics regard themselves as a distinctive community and are accepted as such by the rest of the community." Kelsey William Stuart, author of the 1982 *Newspaperman's Guide to the Law* (in South Africa), commented that in practice "what is considered undesirable" included "pictures and stories about the intermingling of Whites and members of other racial groups and material likely to cause disharmony amongst the various racial groups in the Republic." The Internal Security Act of 1982 consolidated much earlier legislation and prohibited any publication that served "as a means for expressing views or conveying information . . . calculated to cause, encourage or foment feelings of hostility between different population groups of the Republic." The government decided that it could not assure anyone who distributed or showed the movie *Cry Freedom* that she or he would not be prosecuted under the Publications Act and the Internal Security Act. (*Cry Freedom* is a dramatization of the life of black South African activist Steven Biko, who was killed in jail by the South African police.) Although South African courts held that "degrading, humiliating, or ignominious" material about a section of the population was illegal under the acts, there is no record of either statute being used to punish the racist articles published by most of South Africa's white press. Hate speech laws coexisted for sixty years with a practice of racism, segregation, and discrimination so extensive that it shocked the world.

Some American civil libertarians have asked whether laws against hate speech do not lead people to ignore the deeper societal problems that underlie such speech. ACLU executive director Ira Glasser points to the fact that 80 percent of the poor in New York City are black and Latino; the unemployment rate for young black men hovers around 40 percent; a large number of black Americans who use or deal in drugs are arrested while the same activities by white Americans are largely ignored; 80 percent of the Americans who die from curable diseases such as bronchitis, asthma, pneumonia, and gallbladder disease are black; and few white Americans advocate spending money on the kind of programs that would eliminate many of these phenomena. Can those who advocate hate speech laws be serious, he asks, "when they suggest that if only we could repress college students and skinheads from *voicing* bigotry, we could reduce bigotry itself?"

This raises the question of exactly what hate speech laws are designed to do. If the goal is to drive hate speech underground, the laws may have some success. If the object is to eliminate the prejudices that produce hate speech, success is unlikely. Critical Race Theorists would reply that the articulation of hate stereotypes reinforces them and that while the society is dealing—or failing to deal—with the problems of subordination, it is unnecessary for people already victimized by racism to be further injured by words that wound. These opposing positions were inherent in the Skokie situation.

A last consideration that arises when considering the difference between speech jurisprudence and speech laws elsewhere has to do with the conditions of democracy. What elements must be present in a society if it is to accept the dangers of democracy, including the danger of unregulated speech? For democracy, with its assumption that the people are free to decide even if they make very wrong decisions, *is* dangerous. And speech, which affects the beliefs that people hold, has as much potential for harm as it does for good.

The American approach emphasizes the need for speech in a democracy and the great damage to the free flow of ideas that can be done when governments are allowed to decide who shall be permitted to say what. Other nations look at human history and argue that unfettered speech has caused a level of misery and injustice that cannot be allowed to be repeated. Germany and France, for example, both forbid the utterance of some Nazi speech. Both have based such laws on a desire to prevent injury to individuals but also to safeguard the two societies from the kinds of horrors that occurred during the Nazi period. They are uncertain of how well their countries would survive unregulated fascist speech. The German minister of the interior noted in 1982 that half of that country's population had grown up after World War II and had no firsthand experience of Nazi rule. Those Germans might be more open to persuasion by Nazi propaganda than people who had lived through the war years. He and other legislators were concerned about a rash of neo-Nazi incidents centering around a claim that reports of the murders of European Jews in the concentration camps were lies. The result was enactment of a 1985 addition to the criminal code, facilitating prosecution of those who espoused the "Auschwitz lie" in public. Just as some Americans speaking of the Holocaust are convinced that "it can't happen here," so many Europeans remember that it did happen there and are frightened at the possibility of history repeating itself.

The problem of whether it *could* happen here—that is, whether the United States enjoys a system so stable that it is unlikely to be threatened by a system of free speech—is central to the discussion. (The question also could be framed as one about whether a democratic society can afford *not* to have a system of free speech: whether the kind of informed decisions "we the people" are called upon to make in a democracy are possible in the absence of a free flow of ideas.) Some of the preconditions would seem to be the rule of law and a written constitution, an independent judiciary, and the existence of private groups devoted to maintaining the system of free speech. The last deserves a moment's thought. One might well argue that rights in general cannot be properly safeguarded if the responsibility for doing so is left entirely to the government and that this is particularly true in the area of speech. The speech that will be found most threatening by any society, after all, is speech that questions the society's assumptions and orthodoxies. Government officials who depend upon the majority for their reelection are unlikely to be supportive of ideas that the majority fears. It was not the government but the National Association for the Advancement of Colored People, among other organizations, that challenged segregation. Groups such as the National Organization for Women raised matters of gender inequality that the government had not addressed. Gay- and lesbian-rights activists, not the government, have attempted to raise the consciousness of Americans about other inequities.

The government of the United States has a tradition of intolerance of ideas that reaches back at least as far as the Alien and Sedition Act of 1798, when criticism of the government and its officials was outlawed. Criminalization of critiques of public policies during World War I has been mentioned in connection with the *Schenck* case. The genesis of the ACLU, as noted, lay in efforts to protect the speech of opponents of American involvement in that war. The ideas of people labeled as "Communists" and "Communist sympathizers" were stifled during the McCarthy era of the 1950s; and government programs such as the Army's Counter-Intelligence Program and the CIA's "Operation Chaos" monitored and amassed files on the peaceful activities of citizens from the 1940s through the 1970s: singer Josephine Baker, actress Jean Seberg, writer E. B. White, painters Georgia O'Keeffe and Alexander Calder, cartoonist Bill Mauldin, the Reverend Martin Luther King Jr., John Lennon, Senator J. William Fulbright, the Southern Christian Leadership Conference, Clergy and Laymen United Against the War, Women Strike for Peace, Young Americans for Freedom, Americans for Democratic Action, and the National Association for the Advancement of Colored People.

The American experience, coupled with the limits on the existence of organizations protective of speech that seem to accompany severe abridgments of speech elsewhere, suggests that such groups may be as important to a democratic polis as is a popularly elected government or the enumeration of rights in a nation's basic legal documents. That certainly was the assumption of the ACLU when it decided to oppose the village of Skokie.

But, critics of American speech jurisprudence ask, can we "afford" it here? The questions remain: has the United States made a reasoned decision, based on American history and political culture, that we can weather even the most undemocratic speech and that it is best for us to absorb whatever hurts come from words that wound? Or is American free speech jurisprudence no more than an accident of the wording of the First Amendment and the role of the Supreme Court in interpreting it? If so, is it the wisest policy for a country with a history of religious bigotry, racism, and sexism?

CHAPTER 10

"Freedom for the Thought
That We Hate"

*I often wonder whether we do not rest our hopes too much upon constitutions,
upon laws and upon courts. These are false hopes; believe me, these are false hopes.
Liberty lies in the hearts of men and women; when it dies there, no constitution, no law,
no court can save it; no constitution, no law, no court can even do much to help it.
While it lives there it needs no constitution, no law, no court to save it.*

JUDGE LEARNED HAND, *The Spirit of Liberty*

The person who defused the Skokie situation, oddly enough, was Frank
Collin. He apparently had his fill of attempting demonstrations in places
where he had no support, and he had insisted since the beginning that his
real goal was to march in Marquette Park. On May 23, aware that if the
laws pending in the state legislature were enacted they would make his
demonstration impossible for the moment, he offered a deal: he would give
up his appearance in Skokie if he received a permit for one in Chicago.

The press release he issued said that cancellation of the demonstration
in Skokie had three conditions: all the relevant Skokie ordinances had to be
struck down; the state government had to defeat the proposed legislation;
the Chicago Park District had to repeal its insurance requirements. "These
demands are reasonable, lawful and irreversable [*sic*]," the press release stated.

Failure on the part of the Skokie authorities, the State legislators and
the Chicago Park District officers to meet these generous requirements
means that those to whom I have extended my hand in reason desire
blood in the streets of Skokie more than they can tolerate the free speech
of American citizens with a radically different point of view. I reaffirm
that our N.S.P.A. will conduct its Skokie demonstration without use of
violence, but should we be physically attacked, we will fight with a
ruthlessness as terrifying as it will be thorough.

State Senators Carroll and Nimrod expressed outrage at the offer and
the statement. "He is not the kind of person you make a deal with," Carroll

said, indicating that he was still pushing the legislature to enact his proposal. The judiciary committee set hearings on the bills for June 6.

The village of Skokie was preparing for June 25, issuing one permit to Collin and another to the Jewish Federation of Metropolitan Chicago for a counterdemonstration. Still hoping against hope, however, the village filed papers with the United States Supreme Court on May 31, asking that the Court stay either the appeals court's ruling against Judge Wosik's injunction or, failing that, the district court's ruling against enforcement of the ordinances.

As the tension continued to mount, churches from many states articulated their solidarity with the village and the survivors. The action of the Wisconsin United Methodist Church on June 4 was typical. Representatives of its approximately 140,000 members unanimously passed a resolution expressing "our deep sorrow for the continuing affliction of anti-Semitism, our repentance for the participation of our ancestors and ourselves in these ghastly sins, and our pledge that with the love of Christ in our hearts for all people, we will witness with our lives and our faith to the end that the Holocaust will never, never recur." Copies of the resolution went not only to Skokie but to organizations such as the American Jewish Congress. The survivors greeted the statements with pleased amazement: for once, they felt, Jews under siege were not alone.

Collin's followers, on the other hand, felt very much alone. They were abandoning ship at a rate that led him to threaten his men with fines of one hundred dollars if they didn't show up in Skokie. At the same time, he repeated his proposal to move the demonstration to Marquette Park.

Skokie had contacted the Justice Department's Community Relations Service in early March, asking for help in planning the best way to handle the demonstration and counterdemonstration; and representatives of the service had already journeyed to the Chicago area to talk to the principals in the situation. Reacting to Collin's offer, the service called a meeting with Collin and Goldberger on June 1 and asked whether Collin would accept an alternate site in Chicago if Marquette Park remained inaccessible. Collin quickly said yes. The site suggested was the plaza outside the downtown Kluczynski Federal Building—a site controlled by the federal government rather than the Chicago Park District.

While the Justice Department, Goldberger, and, eventually, the Federal Protective Service, the local United States attorney's office, and the Chicago police worked on the details of the deal, the Illinois assembly held a two-hour hearing on the two bills proposed by Senators Carroll and Nimrod and passed by the senate. If the Carroll and Nimrod bills were to become law, the house also had to approve them. Carroll's bill was sponsored in the house by Representative Alan Greiman of Skokie; Nimrod's, by Representative Arthur Telcser of Chicago. Erna Gans, referring to "the silence of the world since 1933," urged the house judiciary committee to vote yes on both. Attorney Joel Sprayregen from Chicago, who had been a staff attorney for the Illinois ACLU from 1958 to 1960 and was now vice chairperson of the Jewish United Fund's public affairs committee, argued that the bills could pass constitutional scrutiny. Aryeh Neier flew in from New York to disagree and to explain the reasoning behind the ACLU's approach to free speech.

Surprisingly enough, in a session at which most of the committee's members felt compelled to explain themselves and reassure the public that they did not like Nazis, they voted overwhelmingly against the bills. They made minispeeches about constitutional principles and voted 15–5 against Nimrod's proposal, 16–4 against Carroll's. Representative Anne Willer stated, "I think this bill could have fearful applications." That sentiment was seconded by Representative Roman Kosinski, who thought that the bills, if approved, "will come back to haunt us" by "eroding the principles of Americanism." Some legislators spoke of "hitting a gnat with a howitzer" and of their fear that the bills had "the potential to turn Illinois into a police state." Technically, a majority of the house could override the committee's votes and put the bills on the house floor. Governor Thompson said he would veto them if that happened and if lawyers for the state told him they were unconstitutional.

On June 12 the United States Supreme Court denied Skokie's appeal in *NSPA v. Skokie* per curiam, with Justices Blackmun and Rehnquist dissenting because the Seventh Circuit's decision seemed to them to be in "some tension" with the precedent of *Beauharnais*. On June 13 the state house of representatives voted by votes of 110–56 and 85–61 not to consider either bill. And on June 14 the ACLU held a National Convocation on Free Speech.

The one-day meeting at the New York Hilton, organized largely by president Norman Dorsen, drew an audience of 1,700. Among the speakers at fifteen seminars and a plenary session were Senators Edward Kennedy and Jacob Javits. Aryeh Neier presented the ACLU's view at a panel on Skokie;

civil liberties attorney William Kuntsler, a former member of the board of directors, agreed with the principle of free speech but argued that the ACLU should not waste its resources defending Collin and his ilk. That drew a response from ninety-four-year-old Roger Baldwin, the best known of the ACLU founders and the organization's leader for decades. The ACLU had survived for over fifty years, he said, because of the "integrity" with which it emphasized principle rather than likable clients. The program also featured a debate between former CIA director William Colby and Morton Halperin, future director of the ACLU's Washington office and later still the White House national security advisor, about the right of access to information held by the government.

Free speech awards were presented to authors James Baldwin, E. L. Doctorow, Jerzy Kosinski, Norman Mailer, Arthur Miller, and William Styron. The best-received event, however, may have been the speech given by cartoonist Jules Feiffer at the luncheon in the Grand Ballroom. The Skokie situation and its contemptible neo-Nazi protagonists, he noted, raised several questions for himself and other ACLU members:

> Why can't we come up with a better class of victims? Whatever became of victims like Eugene Debs? Mythic victims. Victims you could hang around with. Who would enhance your status.
>
> Today there is no question but that we have some terrific victims. We have Indians and Chicanos and blacks and government whistle blowers, all very reassuring to those of us who prefer not merely to believe in civil liberties, but would also like to like them. But we also have *bad* victims, victims who are not nice guys, who are not sympathetic, who are Nazis, who are Kluxers, who are pornographers, who are even crooks. Should crooks have civil liberties? I don't like it.

The point was made with humor but the message was clear: "nice" people with popular views usually don't need civil liberties lawyers to defend their First Amendment rights.

A day later Sol Goldstein's lawyer Jerome Torshen filed an emergency petition with United States Supreme Court Justice John Paul Stevens, asking him to halt the pending demonstration until the survivors' case could be heard by the Supreme Court. Justice Stevens denied the petition on June 20. Torshen then submitted the same request to Justice Rehnquist, who also denied it. The Union of Orthodox Rabbis of the Unites States and

Canada, with a membership of more than six hundred, urged Skokie to defy both of them and refuse to give the NSPA permission for its "march." Back in Skokie, Goldstein, in his capacity as cochair of the federation's committee to plan the counterdemonstration, supplied details to the media. Between sixty and one hundred community, religious, and interfaith leaders would "stand in vigil" across the street from the neo-Nazis, he said, "reciting the Kaddish, the Jewish prayer for the dead, and the names of the death camps where six million Jews and five million non-Jews were gassed, burned and slaughtered." A field hospital staffed by volunteer doctors and nurses would be at the counterdemonstration in a medical trailer supplied by a Chicago hospital. The village said that it had arranged for Skokie's 140-person police force and officers from twelve surrounding communities, state troopers, and units of the Illinois National Guard to keep the peace if a march took place. Police in other local suburbs would be on call. Two hundred marshals, most of them off-duty law enforcement officers, would police the counterdemonstration and keep the two groups of demonstrators separate. A one-square-mile area around the village hall would be cordoned off. Governor Thompson promised to send unarmed national guardsmen if Skokie thought they would be needed.

Collin once again repeated his offer to substitute a demonstration in Chicago, saying that he would prefer to march "among white people" rather than to be confronted by the "mob of howling creatures" who would oppose him in Skokie. The JDL's Bonnie Pechter, not satisfied with the possible cancellation of the demonstration in Skokie, went there to announce that if the NSPA didn't come to Skokie her group would march on Rockwell Hall. "It's time we stop treating them on a nice, polite, intellectual Jewish level," she told reporters. "Nazis are afraid of one thing—landing in the hospital."

An ad hoc coalition of forty Chicago ethnic group leaders, lead by a Ukrainian American, called the proposed NSPA rally "a problem for all Americans." Almost every ethnic group in the country took a position on Skokie. Spokespersons for more than a hundred organizations such as the Latino Institute, the national and the Chicago Urban Leagues, the NAACP, Operation Push, and the National Conference of Christians and Jews promised that those groups would join the counterdemonstration in Skokie. So did Governor Thompson, who said he still intended to be there in spite of a back problem. One thousand residents of Los Angeles were expected to arrive on chartered flights. The tension level went higher every day.

On June 21, Judge George Leighton told Chicago that it had to let Collin march.

David Goldberger had filed a motion for a contempt citation against the Chicago Park District because of its changing its insurance requirement to $60,000 rather than eliminating it entirely. Judge Leighton's first formal action on June 21 was to deny the motion on a technicality. He then invited Goldberger to enter another motion asking that the injunction be modified to cover the new amount and promised to act on it as an "emergency matter." Goldberger complied. When the hearing was held that afternoon, an angry Leighton said that if he had thought the park district would resort to "manipulating" insurance figures he would have issued a broader injunction; and he ordered district officials to allow a demonstration without an insurance requirement in Marquette Park on July 9. "I think it's fair to say that if you require this plaintiff to put up even a $1 insurance policy before he can demonstrate in the park, he couldn't get one," Leighton said. "No company will sell him one. . . . Oh, he might get a $1 policy, I suppose." "If he puts up the dollar," Goldberger remarked. Collin triumphantly continued to milk the story by declining to say until the following day whether he would cancel the demonstration in Skokie.

June 22 found the NSPA leader in his office at Rockwell Hall, seated in front of a swastika-covered flag. Kahane and a few other JDL members shouted outside. The seven brown-uniformed storm troopers clustered around Collin were easily outnumbered by the crush of journalists at the 6 P.M. press conference. The Skokie demonstration, he told reporters, had been "pure agitation on our part to restore our free speech." The "agitation has been successful," he proclaimed. He could now march in Chicago and had no intention of going to Skokie. The NSPA would march at Federal Building Plaza on June 24. Playing to the headlines, he added that if the JDL marched on Rockwell Hall, he and "his people" would "defend our headquarters to the last Jew." Earlier that day police near Rockwell Hall had encountered a man carrying a gasoline can, who had told them he was going to burn the place down. Collin commented that he had given his troops "shoot to kill orders" if there was any attempt to damage the building.

David Smerling, president of the public affairs committee, immediately announced cancellation of the June 25 counterdemonstration in Skokie. Mayor Smith stood on the steps of the village hall to declare that he was revoking the NSPA's permit to march. He too declared success: "I consider this decision a victory for the American way of life and a victory for the freedoms guaranteed by our forefathers." The drama was not yet over, however. The New York City Jewish Community Relations Council said that it, the Catholic Archdiocese of New York, and the Council of Churches of the City of New York would hold an anti-Nazi rally on June 25 at the United States Customs House in Bowling Green Park Plaza, even though the Nazi march in Skokie was off: "We will not be subject to the manipulation of Nazis as to when we speak out." The JDL agreed, promising to send up to four thousand people to use all means, including violence, to stop the Nazis from marching in Chicago. Rabbi Jay Karzen of Des Plaines scheduled a peaceful interfaith demonstration for Sunday, June 25. Other cities and towns made similar plans. In Chicago, Raphael Ortiz, spokesperson for the United Committee Against Injustice, announced that he would bring spectators at the third annual Puerto Rican parade on Michigan Avenue that began at one o'clock on June 24 to the plaza for a counterdemonstration against the NSPA. The Reverend C. H. Turner, chair of the Martin Luther King, Jr. Coalition, promised that coalition members would also be there. The national commander of the Jewish War Veterans promised that three thousand to four thousand members of his organization would stage a vigil outside Rockwell Hall right before the counterdemonstration in Skokie.

———

Counterdemonstrators from around the country had arrived in Chicago by Friday, June 23. Several hundred JDL members came from New York City. Television crews appeared from as far away as Israel. Those who got to Chicago early enough could watch about forty members of the Association of Young Lithuanian Americans demonstrate outside Rockwell Hall. Collin went outside to confront them and was shoved up against a car for a moment.

June 24 was a bright, sunny Saturday in Chicago, but at least part of the city was geared up for a small war. Police officers blanketed the plaza of the Federal Building downtown; hundreds more had their time off canceled and were on standby duty. By 4:30, when the NSPA march was scheduled to begin, several thousand counterdemonstrators lined the plaza.

The JDL's Rabbi Kahane wasn't there, allegedly because it was the Jewish Sabbath. That didn't deter other JDL members or those from the Revolutionary Socialist League, the Black and White Defense Committee, and the Brooklyn, New York, Jewish Athletic League. There were, however, no Nazis in sight. Collin and about twenty followers arrived an hour and a half later, emerging, with a police escort, from an "escape route" through buildings and underground passageways. Greeted by spectators with a hail of eggs, beer cans, rocks, and epithets, the Nazis stayed for only ten or fifteen minutes before leaving the way they had come. Police arrested about a dozen counterdemonstrators and everyone else went home. The first of the two planned marches in Chicago was over.

The march on July 9 was similar, if less well attended. Counterdemonstrators gathered some blocks away from Marquette Park for a march of their own. Among them was a young woman with a bullhorn making a speech about "decent health care" and the "millions of dollars" that were being spend "to kill workers in Chile." A young man, also equipped with a bullhorn, chanted "Hell no, we won't go," the slogan of anti–Vietnam War demonstrators. Others in the crowd chimed in, "Asian, Latin, black and white, workers of the world unite." Police moved the counterdemonstrators away and then refused to let them march to the park as a group. The ACLU would respond by bringing suit on their behalf.

The Nazis also had their supporters. They gathered at the park, some wearing "White Power" T-shirts and yelling, "Jews go home" and "Let the niggers live in Skokie." Most supporters appeared to be from local neighborhoods. In reply, a group of Jewish counterdemonstrators cried, "Never again." Most members of the crowd of about two thousand quietly watched the sideshow as they waited for the main event.

Then Collin, St. Louis Nazi leader Michael Allen, and about twenty-five uniformed followers appeared. The crowd drowned out the speeches the two leaders attempted to make. The several hundred plainclothes officers present broke up a few fights and charged seventy-two people with disorderly conduct.

The NSPA announced plans for demonstrations in several other Chicago suburbs; but after only three members showed up for one demonstration in Lansing that was virtually ignored by the press, it canceled the others.

Collin disappeared from the media. He resurfaced early in 1980, when he was arrested by Chicago police for sexual activities with five boys, aged ten to fifteen, in Rockwell Hall and a local hotel. Apparently paying them for oral sex and taking pornographic pictures of them had been his major activity in 1979, other than working as an orderly at St. Francis Hospital— a job he had taken because the NSPA could no longer afford to support him. The party had ejected him in November 1979 for being "burned out," but the decision reportedly was based on the discovery that he had been using Rockwell Hall for his illicit pastime. He was convicted on eight counts of taking indecent liberties with children and sentenced to seven years in the Pontiac Correctional Center. While in the maximum security facility, he frequently requested and was given protective custody, as prison inmates are not known for their tolerance of child molesters.

Released after three years, Collin gave up his last name in favor of "Frank Joseph" and shucked off his swastikas. He became a proponent of the theory that contact between the Old and the New Worlds existed before Columbus, visited a burial site in Winconsin along with half a dozen white-robed women, and wrote a book entitled *Atlantis in Wisconsin*. He told a Chicago newspaper, "I'm not into [being a neo-Nazi] anymore."

On October 16, 1978, the United State Supreme Court refused to review Decker's and the Seventh Circuit's rulings in the case of the three ordinances. Justices Harry Blackmun and Byron White dissented because of what they saw as the conflict of Judge Decker's decision with *Beauharnais* and a need to delineate the limits to free speech. Blackmun's opinion quoted Judge Robert Sprecher of the Seventh Circuit, who had noted that every court that had dealt with the Skokie cases "feels the need to apologize for its result." (Sprecher had dissented in part because he thought the ordinance requiring an insurance bond was constitutional.) The Supreme Court also denied certiorari in the *Goldstein* case.

The ACLU had won, but victory was somewhat less than sweet. The organization was left with its principles, an attenuated membership, and a fiscal hole in place of a budget. When Ira Glasser became its new executive director in mid-1978 and saw its financial statement for the first time, he asked in semiserious horror whether public interest groups could declare bankruptcy.

The organization had to recoup, and in the summer of 1978 a small meeting of top ACLU leaders was convened to think of ways for it to do so. The people present decided to find someone who was Jewish, whose name was well known, and who could write a good fund-raising letter. Norman Dorsen thought of Arthur Goldberg, former Supreme Court justice and ambassador to the United Nations. A call to his New York City law office elicited the information that he was out of the country. One of the people at the meeting mused, "Goldberg ... Hmm ... What about Goldberger?"

So in August 1978, the ACLU mailed thousands of copies of a letter from David Goldberger addressed to "My Dear Friend" and asking for a contribution of twenty dollars "right now." "The ACLU is now on the edge of a precipice," Goldberger wrote. If "just thirty thousand staunch friends of civil liberties" sent in a check of that size, however, the ACLU could regain its stability. Goldberger spoke of sharing the "agony" of the Skokie survivors and referred to Aryeh Neier's history with Nazism and the "personal threats" that had been made against Goldberger and other members of the ACLU staff. "But the nazis are not the real issue. The Skokie laws are the real issue." Goldberger went on to describe them, noting that "Skokie has already used the very same law to deny the Jewish War Veterans a permit to parade." "Think of such power in the hands of a racist sheriff," Goldberger suggested, "or a local police department hostile to antiwar demonstrators," or, tacitly reminding his listeners of Watergate, "the wrong kind of President."

The organization's ability to represent "the woman who has been cut off from Medicaid payments for abortion ... the parents of a mentally retarded child rotting in a state institution ... a former government employee whose book on the CIA is being censored ... parents and teachers in a high school that has just banned Kurt Vonnegut and Bernard Malamud from its shelves," or to maintain its lobbying in Washington, had been seriously compromised by the resignation of members. Goldberger asked his recipients "to join with others like yourself all over the country not just to support ACLU but to save it."

The result was astonishing. Five hundred fifty thousand dollars was raised from more than 25,000 people, although the record for an ACLU fund-raising appeal until then was two hundred thousand dollars. Four thousand to six thousand new members had signed up by mid-September, and so had many returning members. Among them was Harvard sociologist David Riesman, the author not only of the famed *Lonely Crowd* but of an earlier article that had defended the kind of laws recently passed by Skokie and struck down by Judge Decker. Riesman was living on a pension and described himself as spending what limited energy he still had on questions of nuclear disarmament. He had let his ACLU membership lapse. "But now that I read of the enormous defection from the ACLU precisely because the organization is doing its job," he wrote to Norman Dorsen, "I wanted to rejoin the ACLU and tell you of my personal support for what has been a courageous course of action." Another returning member told Frank Haiman that he had permitted his membership to lapse a year earlier because of his limited funds and the ACLU's growth in numbers. "Your loss of membership over the issue of First Amendment rights for American Nazis has changed my mind," his letter said. "You may count from now on my continued support as long as you don't allow yourself being pressured into compromising your support of free speech." By the early 1980s the ACLU had a membership well in excess of 200,000. In 1998 it had more than 270,000 members, chapters or affiliates or both in every state, a staff of 105 working in its New York City office and its office in Washington, D.C., and a docket of six thousand cases a year.

––––––

The Nazis did come to Skokie on May 1, 1977. They got no farther than the Skokie exit of the Edens Expressway, however, before local police, acting in accordance with the county courts' injunction, sent them back to Chicago. By the time higher tribunals had validated its right to demonstrate in Skokie, the NSPA had decided that going there might not be wise. The Skokie survivors were nonetheless permanently affected by the reaction to the NSPA's proposed demonstration. They could talk of the difference between the way they had acted in 1977 to 1978 and the response to Nazism in Germany. Sol Goldstein spoke at a memorial service in Skokie on June 25, 1978, for those who died in World War II. The service had been hastily organized in the Niles Jewish Congregation synagogue because two hundred Californians had flown to Skokie in anticipation of a Nazi march there. Referring to the way many Europeans had been forced to act during that war, Goldstein admonished them, "Don't go into your homes. Don't lock the doors. Don't pull the drapes. Don't go into the basement. Evil will triumph only when decent human beings are silent." A crowd that included

African-American leaders such as the Reverend Jesse Jackson listened and cheered. Goldstein turned to them as he continued,

> Yesterday, I was down at the federal building. A black man came up to me. "Are you Jewish?" he asked.
> "Yes," I said.
> "Well, I am with you," he told me.
> "Are you black?" I asked him.
> "Yes," he said.
> "Then," I said, "I am with you too."

The crowd laughed and the service ended with Jewish Americans and African Americans promising to support each other's anti-Nazi demonstrations.

Another of the survivors, quoted by journalist Carolyn Toll two days earlier, shared Goldstein's sentiments. The survivor, paradoxically, was disappointed that the Nazis had not come to Skokie after all: "It is important to show the Nazis that Jews can't be pushed off to the side, hiding in cellars, allowing their leaders to pick which of them will stand up and which will cower in the high school stadium as they did when living under Hitler."

Many survivors, buoyed by the support of people all over the country as well as by Jews and non-Jews alike in Skokie, finally felt free to speak out. "Suddenly, I didn't feel so alone," one woman said. "I realized the whole world was paying attention to Skokie. And thousands of people were behind us." They decided that the town needed a permanent memorial to the millions who had died during the Holocaust. And so, with the village government donating part of the grassy lawn between the village hall and the nearby public library, the survivors raised the money for a searing Holocaust memorial reminding bypassers of what had happened in Europe—and had not occurred in Skokie. It was dedicated in 1987.

Mayor Smith had been elated in the hours after Judge Leighton issued his order to let the Nazis march in Chicago, even before Collin rescheduled his demonstration for Chicago. He viewed all the publicity as having dealt anti-Semitism a blow "like nothing else before." Instead of Collin's gaining stature, Smith thought, "there was a giant backlash." He wondered aloud about what might have occurred had the German non-Jewish population reacted differently to Hitler's anti-Semitic policies. "If this kind of concern had been expressed . . . perhaps the Holocaust might not have happened." The editors of the *Chicago Tribune* responded with an editorial saying that Smith should have added, "[I]f the dissidents in Hitler's Germany had had the freedom to speak out that today's America has given the neo-Nazis, things might have happened in Germany as Mr. Smith wishes they had."

David Hamlin got into his car that summer and drove to California for a month-long and almost newspaperless vacation. He returned to Chicago and announced that he was leaving the ACLU as of October 1978, in part to write a book about Skokie. Aryeh Neier produced his own book on the subject and became executive director of Human Rights Watch, an organization that monitors human rights violations around the world. His successor, Ira Glasser, wrote no book about Skokie but pulled the ACLU out of debt and is now leading it into the twenty-first century. Barbara O'Toole remains a dedicated volunteer attorney for the Illinois ACLU.

David Goldberger had been teaching as an adjunct professor at Kent Law School since 1972. In 1980 he left Chicago for Columbus, Ohio, and a professorship at the Ohio State University College of Law, becoming director of the law school's clinical programs in 1986. While he taught and wrote scholarly articles, Goldberger also served as general counsel of the Ohio ACLU affiliate from 1984 through 1993. In 1980 he received the Hefner Foundation's First Amendment award. In 1994 Goldberger argued and won the case of *McIntyre v. Ohio Elections Commission* (decided in 1995) before the United States Supreme Court. Justice John Paul Stevens declared for a 7–2 court that an Ohio statute prohibiting the distributing of anonymous campaign literature violated the First Amendment. Goldberger was still litigating on behalf of the right to speak.

Frank Haiman, by 1998 a retired professor of communication studies and a California resident, saw a number of good things coming out of Skokie. The press had "seemed to turn in our favor" as the Skokie story unfolded. The decisions by Judge Decker and the federal court of appeals, as left standing by the Supreme Court, changed the law. Legal commentary thereafter indicated that *Beauharnais* and its doctrine of actionable group libel had effectively been overturned. The result of the public debate over the limits of speech meant that "people got better informed about free speech" and that "new people who had been quiet sympathizers but not members joined because the ACLU stood on principle." He might have added that the publicity also gave large numbers of people the opportunity to learn about the Holocaust and the horrendous things that can happen when people forget that differences do not imply inferiority.

Harvey Schwartz became an Illinois judge in 1987 and served until his retirement at the end of 1996. Looking back in 1997, he commented, "The survivors won their battle, the village of Skokie . . . whenever we travelled, we always were treated a little bit like celebrities because we were from Skokie. . . . 'Oh, you're from that community that kept out the Nazis.'"

He was no longer certain, however, that the cause of free speech would have won had Skokie been successful in court. "Who knows what would have happened?" he wondered. He had received calls afterwards from attorneys in other villages "who had to then deal not only with the Nazis but with the KKK and others. Had we won that case, there certainly would have been different lines drawn." "Sure, maybe we're doing the right thing for the moment . . . ," he mused aloud. "It was my argument that you could distinguish Skokie," and he was proud of the way he and others in Skokie had reacted. The precedent the Skokie case could have set, however, would have jeopardized the meaning of the First Amendment: "[C]ertainly insofar as lawyers citing it [the precedent that could have been established] for various rhymes and reasons, why, it would have offered a real challenge."

And if that had happened, perhaps it would not have been a good day for free speech in the United States.

CHRONOLOGY

1914	Sol Goldstein born in Minsk, Russia.
1929	Harvey Schwartz born in United States.
1937	Aryeh Neier born in Berlin, Germany.
June 22, 1941	World War II reaches Kovno, Lithuania.
July 10, 1941	Creation of the Kovno ghetto.
1941	David Goldberger born in United States.
1945	Frank Collin born in United States.
1968	David Goldberger becomes staff attorney for the Illinois ACLU.
June 1976	A federal district court judge in Chicago finds the city's requirement of a parade insurance bond to be unconstitutional in a case brought by the Illinois ACLU on behalf of Frank Collin *(Collin v. O'Malley)*; the city immediately appeals.
October 1976	Frank Collin sends letters to park districts in suburbs north of Chicago asking for permission to demonstrate. Only Skokie replies, saying it requires posting of a $350,000 bond.
March 20, 1977	Frank Collin writes to the Skokie Park District that the NSPA plans to demonstrate on May 1, claiming that the bond requirement violates the First Amendment.
March–April	Responding to Collin's request, survivors and sympathizers meet in Skokie and nearby suburbs.
April 27	Skokie files for an injunction against the proposed demonstration; Collin contacts David Goldberger of the Illinois ACLU; Goldberger and O'Toole meet to prepare for the case.
April 28	Schwartz and Goldberger argue *Skokie v. NSPA* in Judge Wosik's courtroom. Wosik grants the injunction for May 1.
April 29	David Goldberger appeals to the Illinois Appellate Court for a stay of the injunction; court denies it. Collin then announces he will march on April 30 instead of May 1.
April 30	In an emergency hearing, Skokie is granted an alteration of the original injunction to include April 30 and all dates thereafter. Collin and NSPA members turn back from Skokie.

May 2	Skokie's mayor and city council pass three ordinances designed to prevent the NSPA from demonstrating in Skokie.
May 4	Board of directors of Illinois ACLU votes unanimously to take the Collin case. Goldberger and O'Toole subsequently file a motion in federal district court to have the three ordinances overturned as a violation of the First Amendment *(Collin v. Smith)*.
May 25	Illinois Supreme Court denies Goldberger's appeal from appellate court refusal to stay injunction.
June 14	United States Supreme Court rules *(NSPA v. Skokie)* that the Illinois courts must lift the injunction or hear an argument on the merits immediately and returns the case to the Illinois Supreme Court. The Illinois Supreme Court orders the Illinois Appellate Court to hold a hearing on the merits.
June 22	Collin applies for a permit to hold a demonstration in front of the Skokie village hall on July 4 and asks the village to waive the insurance requirement or help him find an insurer.
June 22	District Court Judge George Leighton hands down a preliminary decision overturning Chicago's parade insurance requirement and temporarily halting its enforcement *(Collin v. O'Malley)*. Chicago appeals.
June 22	Illinois Supreme Court returns the injunction case to the appellate court for a speedy hearing.
June 29	Judge Archibald Carey of Cook Country Circuit Court denies Goldberger's motion to dismiss *Goldstein v. Collin,* the "menticide" case in which Sol Goldstein asks for an injunction against any NSPA demonstration; sets August 29 trial date.
July 2	Collin postpones the July 4 demonstration in Skokie; vows to demonstrate there before the year is out.
July 4	Demonstration in Skokie by Jewish Defense League and other organizations.
July 8	Illinois Appellate Court hears argument on the injunction. On July 12 the court overturns the injunction except for the prohibition on display of the swastika *(Skokie v. NSPA)*.
Dec. 2, 1977	Goldberger and Schwartz argue *Collin v. Smith* before Judge Bernard Decker in federal district court.

January 8, 1978	American Jewish Congress national governing council adopts resolution opposing any NSPA "march" in Skokie if it includes Nazi uniforms and swastikas; says it will file an amicus brief before the United States Supreme Court if the pending decision of the Illinois Supreme Court in the injunction case is appealed.
January 24	Theodore Mann delivers address on AJC position to the National Jewish Community Relations Advisory Council.
January 27	Illinois Supreme Court strikes down the entire injunction *(Skokie v. NSPA)*; simultaneously dismisses *Goldstein v. Collin.*
February 23	Decker strikes down the three ordinances *(Collin v. Smith).*
March 11	NSPA demonstration in St. Louis.
March 13	Collin announces the NSPA will march in Skokie on April 20, Hitler's birthday; subsequently changes date to April 22, the first day of Passover.
March 8	Jewish United Fund of Chicago's public affairs committee announces plans for a counterdemonstration in Skokie. By the end of the month, thirty-four major Chicago Jewish organizations are involved.
March 16	Skokie moves to delay the effective date of Decker's ruling until the federal Court of Appeals for the Seventh Circuit hears and decides the case.
March 17	Decker grants the delay for forty-five days.
March 31	Three-judge panel of the Seventh Circuit Court of Appeals denies Goldberger's request to vacate Decker's stay and sets oral argument in *Collin v. Smith;* April 5, announces that the entire eight-judge court will reconsider the ruling; April 6, upholds stay for thirty days and schedules oral argument for April 14.
April 11	Collin sends Skokie an application for a permit to demonstrate on June 25.
April 14	Goldberger and Schwartz argue *Collin v. Smith* before three-judge panel of the court of appeals.
May 2	Illinois Senate judiciary committee unanimously endorses bills introduced by Senators Howard W. Carroll and John Nimrod that would criminalize "public display of racial hatred" and permit any potentially affected party to apply for an injunction against such display.

May 10	Illinois Senate passes Carroll and Nimrod bills.
May 22	Court of Appeals agrees with Decker, in *Collin v. Smith,* that the three ordinances are unconstitutional.
May 26	Skokie issues Collin a permit to demonstrate on June 25.
May 30	Skokie issues the Jewish Federation of Metropolitan Chicago a permit for a counterdemonstration on June 25.
June 6	Illinois House judiciary committee votes down Carroll and Nimrod bills.
June 12	United States Supreme Court denies Skokie's appeal in *NSPA v. Skokie.*
June 13	Illinois House of Representatives votes down Carroll and Nimrod bills.
June 14	ACLU National Convention on Free Speech.
June 21	Judge Leighton orders Chicago to permit Collin to demonstrate *(Collin v. O'Malley).* Collin announces the NSPA won't demonstrate in Skokie.
June 24	NSPA marches in Federal Plaza, Chicago.
June 25	Memorial service in Skokie for Holocaust victims.
July 9	NSPA rally in Marquette Park, Chicago.
August	ACLU sends out Goldberger fund-raising letter.
Oct. 16	United States Supreme Court denies certiorari, *Smith v. Collin* and *Goldstein v. Collin.*
April 1980	Frank Collin goes to jail for molesting minors.
1987	Holocaust memorial is dedicated in Skokie.

RELEVANT CASES

Abrams v. United States (1919), 250 U.S. 616 (1919).

American Booksellers Association v. Hudnut, 475 U.S. 1001 (1986).

Barron v. Baltimore, 32 U.S. 243 (1833).

Beauharnais v. Illinois, 343 U.S. 250 (1952).

Better Austin v. Keefe, 402 U.S. 415 (1971).

Board of Education v. Barnette, 319 U.S. 624 (1943).

Brandenburg v. Ohio, 395 U.S. 444 (1969).

Brown v. Board of Education (1964), 347 U.S. 483 (1954).

Butler v. the Queen, 1 S.C.R. 452 (Can. 1992).

Cantwell v. Connecticut, 310 U.S. 296 (1940).

Chaplinsky v. New Hampshire, 315 U.S. 568 (1942).

Cohen v. California, 403 U.S. 15 (1971).

Dambrot v. Central Michigan University, 839 F. Supp. 477 (E.D. Mich. 1993).

Doe v. University of Michigan, 721 F. Supp. 852 (E.D. Mich. 1989).

Erznoznik v. City of Jacksonville, 422 U.S. 205 (1975).

Feiner v. New York, 340 U.S. 315 (1951).

Geduldig v. Aiello, 417 U.S. 484 (1974).

General Electric v. Gilbert, 429 U.S. 124 (1976).

Gertz v. Robert Welch, Inc., 418 U.S. 323 (1974).

Gitlow v. New York, 268 U.S. 652 (1925).

Gooding v. Wilson, 405 U.S. 515 (1972).

Kimmerle v. New York, 262 U.S. 99 (1933).

Lewis v. City of New Orleans, 415 U.S. 130 (1974).

Marbury v. Madison, 5 U.S. (1 Cranch) 137 (1803).

McIntyre v. Ohio Elections Commission, 514 U.S. 334 (1995).

Murdock v. Pennsylvania, 319 U.S. 105 (1943).

Near v. Minnesota, 283 U.S. 697 (1943).

Nebraska Press Association v. Stuart, 427 U.S. 539 (1976).

New York Times v. Sullivan, 376 U.S. 254 (1964).

R.A.V. v. City of St. Paul, 505 U.S. 377 (1992).

Rockwell v. Morris, 10 N.Y.2d 721, 166 N.E.1d 48 (1961).

Rosenbloom v. Metromedia, Inc., 403 U.S. 29 (1971).

Schenck v. United States, 249 U.S. 47 (1919).

Stromberg v. California, 283 U.S. 359 (1931).

Terminiello v. Chicago, 337 U.S. 1 (1949).

Thornhill v. Alabama, 310 U.S. 88 (1940).

Tinker v. Des Moines School District, 393 U.S. 503 (1969).

United States v. Carolene Products, 304 U.S. 144 (1938).

United States v. O'Brien, 391 U.S. 367 (1968).

United States v. Schwimmer, 279 U.S. 644 (1929).

UWM Post v. Board of Regents of the University of Wisconsin, 774 F. Supp. 1163 (E.D. Wis. 1991).

West Virginia State Board of Education v. Barnette, 319 U.S. 624 (1943).

Whitney v. California, 274 U.S. 357 (1927).

Skokie cases:

The case in which Skokie asked for an injunction against any demonstration by the NSPA and in which the Illinois Appellate and Supreme Courts denied a stay of it is *Skokie v. NSPA*, 69 Ill. 2d 605, 373 N.E.2d 21 (1977). The U.S. Supreme Court's decision ordering a hearing on the merits is *NSPA v. Skokie*, 432 U.S. 43 (1977). The Illinois Appellate Court's upholding of the ban against swastikas is *Skokie v. NSPA*, 51 Ill. Supl. 3d 279, N.E. 2d 347 (1977); the Illinois Supreme Court's overturning of the ban, *Skokie v. NSPA*, 69 Ill. 2d 605, 373 N.E.2d 21 (1978). Collin's suit against the three ordinances is *Collin v. Smith*, 447 F. Supp. 676 (N.D. Ill., 1977); 578 F.2d 1197 (1978) (7th Cir.); *Smith v. Collin*, cert. den., 439 U.S. 916 (1978). Collin challenged the Chicago Park District's bond requirement in *Collin v. O'Malley*, 452 F. Supp. 577 (1978). The menticide case is *Goldstein v. Collin*, cert. den., 439 U.S. 910 (1978).

BIBLIOGRAPHICAL ESSAY

Note from the Series Editors: The following bibliographical essay contains the primary and secondary sources the author consulted for this volume. We have asked all authors in the series to omit formal citations in order to make our volumes more readable, inexpensive, and appealing for students and general readers. In adopting this format, Landmark Law Cases and American Society follows the precedent of a number of highly regarded and widely consulted series.

There are so many works on speech philosophy and jurisprudence, the history of speech law, and the question of hate speech that this list necessarily presents only a sampling. An update on current speech and assembly issues can be found on the First Amendment Cyber-Tribune's site on the World Wide Web at http://w.3.trib.com/FACT/ (click on freedom of speech or freedom to assemble). Also see the ACLU's www.aclu.org/issues/freespeech/ for its approach to current issues.

One of the more important volumes presenting the reasons for and the history of free speech in the United States is Thomas I. Emerson, *Toward a General Theory of the First Amendment* (Random House, 1966); revised as *The System of Freedom of Expression* (Random House, 1970). Also see Harry Kalven, *A Worthy Tradition: Freedom of Speech in America* (Harper & Row, 1988), and *The Negro and the First Amendment* (University of Chicago, 1965); Lee C. Bollinger, *The Tolerant Society: Freedom of Speech and Extremist Speech in America* (Oxford University Press, 1986); and Rodney A. Smolla, *Free Speech in an Open Society* (Knopf, 1992). Franklyn Haiman, *Speech and Law in a Free Society* (University of Chicago, 1981), presents the traditional civil liberties view of speech. Haiman's *"Speech Acts" and the First Amendment* (Southern Illinois University Press, 1993), addresses the issue of symbolic speech. The view that speech should be protected only if it is consistent with classical Greek notions of virtue and justice illuminates Walter Berns, *Freedom, Virtue, and the First Amendment* (Louisiana State University Press, 1957); also see his *The First Amendment and the Failure of American Democracy* (Basic Books, 1976). Mark A. Graber, *Transforming Free Speech: The Ambiguous Legacy of Civil Libertarianism* (University of California Press, 1991), discusses the philosophical and constitutional foundations and history of the right to free speech in the United States. Among other volumes worth consulting is Owen M. Fiss, *The Irony of Free Speech* (Harvard University Press, 1996), which challenges the traditional presumption that the state is the natural enemy of free speech by contrasting the individualistic "libertarian" view of speech with "democratic theory." Fiss's *Liberalism Divided: Freedom of Speech and the Many Uses of State Power* (Westview Press, 1996), contains some of his essays as well as the Indiana pornography statute and the decision in *R.A.V. v. City of St. Paul*. One expression of the opposing view is Ronald K. L. Collins and David M. Skover, *The Death of Discourse* (Westview Press, 1996). Paul

A. Passavant, "A Moral Geography of Liberty: John Stuart Mill and American Free Speech Discourse," 5 *Social & Legal Studies* 301 (1996), provides information about a theorist influential to American speech jurisprudence.

The history of the rights of speech and press is traced in Leonard Levy, *Legacy of Suppression* (Harvard University Press, 1960); *Emergence of a Free Press* (Oxford University Press, 1985); and *Freedom of Speech and Press in Early American History: Legacy of Suppression* (Harper & Row, 1960). Paul Murphy, *World War I and the Origin of Civil Liberties in the United States* (Norton, 1979), treats that important period. David M. Rabban, *Free Speech in Its Forgotten Years* (Cambridge University, 1997), covers speech legislation and jurisprudence before and during the First World War years. Also see his "The Free Speech League, the ACLU, and Changing Conceptions of Free Speech in American History," 45 *Stanford Law Review* 47 (1992), and G. Edward White, "The First Amendment Comes of Age: The Emergence of Free Speech in Twentieth-Century America," 95 *Michigan Law Review* (1996), which covers almost all of the century. Among the volumes tracing history and cases handled by the Supreme Court are Philip Kurland, ed., *Free Speech and Association: The Supreme Court and the First Amendment* (University of Chicago, 1975); David S. Bogen, *Bulwark of Liberty: the Court and the First Amendment* (Associated Faculty Press, 1984); James E. Leahy, *The First Amendment, 1791–1991: Two Hundred Years of Freedom* (McFarland & Co., 1991); and Jethro K. Lieberman, *Free Speech, Free Press, and the Law* (Lothrop, Lee & Shepard, 1980). Louis E. Ingelhart, *Press and Speech Freedoms in America, 1619–1995: A Chronology* (Greenwood Press, 1997), contains cases and quotes from Supreme Court justices as well as information about the impact of technology on speech jurisprudence.

The fighting words doctrine after *Chaplinsky* is the subject of Gard, "Fighting Words as Free Speech," 58 *Washington University Law Quarterly* 531 (1980); Shea, "'Don't Bother to Smile When You Call Me That'—Fighting Words and the First Amendment," 63 *Kentucky Law Journal* 1 (1975); and Kent Greenawalt, *Fighting Words: Individuals, Communities, and Liberties of Speech* (Princeton University Press, 1995). Also see *Gooding v. Wilson*, 504 U.S. 515 (1972).

Hate in the Ivory Tower (People for the American Way, 1990), is a survey of intolerant acts on college campuses during the 1980s and the varying institutional responses to it. Monroe H. Freedman and Eric M. Freedman, eds., *Group Defamation and Freedom of Speech: The Relationship between Language and Violence* (Greenwood Press, 1995), includes essays by Kenneth Clark, Michael Blain, Mari Matsuda, Lee Bollinger, Catharine A. MacKinnon, and others. It also has the top entries in a student contest to draft a model group-defamation statute and a hypothetical court's opinions, written by the editors, based on the winning entry. David Riesman, "Democracy and Defamation: Control of Group Libel," 42 *Columbia Law Review* 727 (1942), similarly calls for limitations on hate speech. Milton Heumann and Thomas Church with David Relawsk, eds., *Hate Speech on Campus: Cases, Case Studies and Commentary* (Northeastern University Press, 1997), contains cases such as *Schenck, Whitney, Brandenburg,* and *Cohen;* five campus hate speech code case studies; and selections by speech theorists such as John Stuart Mill, Herbert Marcuse, and Charles Lawrence.

Henry Louis Gates Jr. et al., *Speaking of Race, Speaking of Sex: Hate Speech, Civil Rights, and Civil Liberties* (New York University Press, 1994), has articles in favor of and against campus hate speech codes, as does the Public Agenda Foundation's extremely accessible *The Boundaries of Free Speech: How Free is Too Free?* (McGraw-Hill, 1992). Gara LaMarche, ed., *Speech and Equality: Do We Really Have to Choose?* (New York University Press, 1996), has a section on differing views of "Hate Crimes/Hate Speech" by Ira Glasser, Martin Redish, and Randall Kennedy. Arati R. Kirwar, *War of Words: Speech Codes,* 2d ed. (Freedom Forum First Amendment Center, 1995), summarizes the pro and con arguments and offers a list of campuses with such codes. The major work by Critical Race Theorists is Mari J. Matsuda, Charles R. Lawrence III, Richard Delgado, and Kimberle Williams Crenshaw, *Words That Wound: Critical Race Theory, Assaultive Speech, and the First Amendment* (Westview Press, 1993). It includes articles by each author and a helpful introductory essay. Richard Delgado and Laura Lederer, *The Price We Pay: The Case against Racist Speech, Hate Propaganda, and Pornography* (Hill and Wang, 1995), and Richard Delgado and Jean Stefancic, *Must We Defend Nazis? Hate Speech, Pornography, and the New First Amendment* (New York University Press, 1997), argue in favor of speech codes, as do Patricia Williams in *The Rooster's Egg* (Harvard University Press, 1995); Mary Ellen Gale in "Reimagining the First Amendment: Racist Speech and Equal Liberty," 65 *St. John's Law Review* 119 (1991); David Kretzmer, "Free Speech and Racism," 8 *Cardozo Law Review* 445 (1987); and Cass R. Sunstein, "Liberalism, Speech Codes, and Related Problems," 79 *Academe* 14 (1993). Also see Sunstein, *Democracy and the Problem of Free Speech* (Free Press, 1993), suggesting that government regulation of speech to make democratic debate more robust may be desirable. There is a variety of essays on both sides in Steven J. Heyman, ed., *Hate Speech and the Constitution* (Garland Press, 1996).

The phrase "words that wound" is taken from Richard Delgado, "Words That Wound: A Tort Action for Racial Insults, Epithets, and Name Calling," 17 *Harvard Civil Rights–Civil Liberties Law Review* 133 (1982). Delgado's "Campus Antiracism Rules: Constitutional Narratives in Collision," 85 *Northwest University Law Review* (1991), discusses the limits on speech that United States courts have accepted as reasonable. Nicholas Wolfson makes the opposing argument in *Hate Speech, Sex Speech, Free Speech* (Praeger 1997), and charges that proponents of the codes have lost faith in the marketplace of ideas. Also see Robert A. Sedler, "The Unconstitutionality of Campus Bans on 'Racist Speech,'" 53 *University of Pittsburgh Law Review* 543 (1992), and Marjorie Heins, "Banning Words: A Comment on 'Words That Wound,'" 18 *Harvard Civil Rights–Civil Liberties Law Review* 585 (1983).

There is a good history of speech codes at various universities, as well as an anticode conclusion, in "Closing the Campus Gates to Free Expression: The

Regulation of Offensive Speech at Colleges and Universities," 39 *Emory Law Journal* 1351 (1990). The traditional civil liberties/ACLU approach to speech is presented in Samuel Walker, *Hate Speech: The History of an American Controversy* (University of Nebraska Press, 1994), and Nadine Strossen, "Regulating Racist Speech on Campus: A Modest Proposal?" 1990 *Duke Law Journal* 484 (1990). Charles Lawrence, a Critical Race Theorist, takes the opposite point of view in the same journal: "If He Hollers Let Him Go: Regulating Racist Speech on Campus," 1990 *Duke Law Journal* 431 (1990), also reprinted in *Words That Wound.* The argument that prohibition of hate speech does nothing to alleviate the problem of societal discrimination and that colleges should educate their communities about it is made in Katharine T. Bartlett and Jean O'Barr, "The Chilly Climate on College Campus: An Expansion of the 'Hate Speech' Debate," 1990 *Duke Law Journal* 574 (1990).

Charles H. Jones, "Equality, Dignity and Harm: The Constitutionality of Regulating American Campus Ethnoviolence," 37 *Wayne Law Review* 1383 (1991), is an attempt to find a middle ground. *Free Speech in the College Community* by Robert M. O'Neil (Indiana University Press, 1997) is written as memos from one university official to another, laying out the problems of maintaining campus peace while not violating the First Amendment. It does not offer suggestions for resolving the issue. The international perspective on hate speech is summarized in Elizabeth F. Defeis, "Freedom of Speech and International Norms: A Response To Hate Speech," 29 *Stanford Journal of International Law* 57 (1992). See also "Symposium, Language as Violence v. Freedom of Expression: Canadian and American Perspectives on Group Defamation," 37 *Buffalo Law Review* 337 (1989).

Answers to Critical Legal Studies and Critical Race Theory arguments can be found in Mark A. Graber, "Old Wine in New Bottles," 48 *Vanderbilt Law Review* 348 (1995); C. Edwin Baker, "Of Course, More than Words," 61 *University of Chicago Law Review* 1181 (1994); and Jeffrey Rosen, "The Limits of Limits," *New Republic,* February 7, 1994. The communitarian theory of speech is in Michael J. Sandel, *Democracy's Discontent: America in Search of a Public Philosophy* (Harvard University Press, 1996); also see Sandel, *Liberalism and the Limits of Justice* (Cambridge University Press, 1982), Amitai Etzioni, *Rights and the Common Good: The Communitarian Perspective* (St. Martin's Press, 1995); Etzioni, *The Spirit of Community: Rights, Responsibilities, and the Communitarian Agenda* (Crown Publishers, 1993).

Allan C. Hutchinson, ed., *Critical Legal Studies* (Rowman, 1988), is an excellent overview to that school of thought. A good introduction to Critical Race Theory and Critical Feminist Legal Theory is Stephen M. Griffin and Robert C. L. Moffat, eds., *Radical Critiques of the Law* (University of Kansas, 1997); also see Patricia Smith, ed., *Feminist Jurisprudence* (Oxford University Press, 1993). For the feminist school of legal theory that favors restricting speech, see Catharine A. MacKinnon, *Only Words* (Harvard University Press, 1993), and *Toward a Feminist Theory of the State* (Harvard, 1989); Martha Minow, *Making All the Difference* (Cornell University Press, 1990); and Cynthia V. Ward, "A Kinder, Gentler Liberalism? Visions of Empathy in Feminist and Communitarian Literature," 61 *University of Chicago Law Review* 929 (1994).

Ronald J. Berger et al., *Feminism and Pornography* (Praeger, 1991), presents opposing views about pornography and speech. Donald A. Downs, *The New Politics of Pornography* (University of Chicago Press, 1989), includes an examination of the Minneapolis and Indianapolis ordinances. Paul Brest and Ann Vandenberg, "Politics, Feminism, and the Constitution: The Anti-Pornography Movement in Minneapolis," 39 *Stanford Law Review* 607 (1987), details the background of the MacKinnon proposal. Also see Andrew M. Jacobs, "Rhetoric and the Creation of Rights: MacKinnon and the Civil Right to Freedom From Pornography," 42 *Kansas Law Review* 785 (1994), and Gordon Hawkins and Franklin Zimring, *Pornography in a Free Society* (Cambridge University Press, 1988). Frank I. Michelman, "Conceptions of Democracy in American Constitutional Argument: The Case of Pornography Regulation," 56 *Tennessee Law Review* 291 (1989), takes the position that pornography subordinates and silences women. Andrea Dworkin, *Pornography: Men Possessing Women* (Putman, 1981) presents a radical feminist analysis of pornography and defines male sex as dominance and violence. Catharine A. MacKinnon's views are explicated in "Feminist, Marxism, Method, and the State: Toward Feminist Jurisprudence," 8 *Signs* 635 (1983), and "Pornography, Civil Rights, and Speech," 20 *Harvard Civil Rights–Civil Liberties Law Review* 1 (1985), in addition to the books mentioned earlier. Also see Susan H. Williams, "Feminist Jurisprudence and Free Speech Theory," 68 *Tulane Law Review* 1563 (1994).

The opposing feminist view of free speech as necessary to gender equality is presented by Nadine Strossen (current ACLU president) in "A Feminist Critique of 'The' Feminist Critique of Pornography," 79 *Virginia Law Review* 1099 (1993), and *Defending Pornography: Free Speech, Sex, and the Fight for Women's Rights* (Scribner, 1995). For the views of the Feminist Anti-Censorship Taskforce, see Nan D. Hunter and Sylvia A. Law, *"American Booksellers v. Hudnut,"* 21 *University of Michigan Journal of Law* 69 (1987–1988). The feminist anticensorship view appears also in Kate Ellis et al., eds., *Caught Looking: Feminism, Pornography and Censorship* (Real Comet Press, 1988). Similar views are expressed in Ronald Dworkin, "Women and Pornography," *New York Review of Books,* October 21, 1993, and Henry Louis Gates, Jr., "Let Them Talk," *New Republic,* September 20 and 27, 1993.

Canadian feminist anticensorship activists speak out in a collection of essays edited by Varda Burstyn, *Women against Censorship* (Douglas and McIntyre, 1985). Marie-France Major contrasts the two countries in "Obscene Comparisons: Canadian and American Attitudes Toward Pornography Regulation," 19 *Journal of Contemporary Law* 51 (1993). For a view of the impact of free speech on the gay- and lesbian-rights movement, see H. N. Hirsch, "Levels of Scrutiny, The First Amendment, and Gay Rights," forthcoming in 7 Tulane *Journal of Law and Sexuality* (1998).

Richard B. Lillich, *International Human Rights Instruments: A Compilation of Treaties, Agreements and Declarations* (W. S. Hein Co., 1990), contains the relevant international instruments such as the 1966 International Covenant on Civil and Political Rights, 1950 European Convention for the Protection of Human Rights and Fundamental Freedoms, 1965 International Convention on the Elimination of All Forms of Racial Discrimination, 1981 Declaration on the Elimination of All Forms of Intolerance and of Discrimination Based on Religion or Belief, 1979 Convention on Discrimination Against Women, 1969 American Convention on Human Rights, and 1981 African Charter on Human and Peoples' Rights, as do many basic international human rights law textbooks. There is a chart showing which countries subscribe to which international instruments in Article 19, *The Article 19 Freedom of Expression Handbook* (Bath Press, 1993). Sandra Coliver, ed., *Striking a Balance: Hate Speech, Freedom of Expression and Non-discrimination* (Article 19, 1992) presents a similar survey. Ilan Peleg, ed., *Patterns of Censorship around the World* (Westview Press, 1993) contains essays about speech jurisprudence in a variety of countries. The pre-Mandela South African laws are discussed in D. S. K. Culhane, "'No Easy Talk': South Africa and the Suppression of Political Speech," 17 *Fordham International Law Journal* (1994) and J. C. W. Van Rooyen, "Censorship," in W. A. Joubert, *The Law of South Africa*, v. 2 (Butterworths, 1976). Donald P. Kommers, "The Jurisprudence of Free Speech in the U.S. and the Federal Republic of Germany," 53 *Southern California Law Review* 657, and Eric Stein, "History against Free Speech: The New German Law against the 'Auschwitz'—and Other—'Lies,'" 85 *Michigan Law Review* 277 (1986), discuss the German experience. The British experience is addressed in W. J. Wolffe, "Values in Conflict: Incitement to Racial Hatred and the Public Order Act 1986," 1987 *Public Law* 85 (1987), and David Bonner and Richard Stone, "The Public Order Act 1986: Steps in the Wrong Direction?" 1987 *Public Law* 202 (1987). Eliezer Lederman and Mala Tabory, "Criminalization of Legal Incitement in Israel," 24 *Stanford Journal of International Law* 55–84 (1987), is critical of Israel's restrictions on hate speech; Marc E. Bernstein, "Freedom of Speech in the Israeli Occupied Territories: The Search for a Standard," 21 *International Law and Politics* 553 (1989), takes an opposing position.

Various United States Supreme Court justices have addressed the issue of speech jurisprudence. Interested readers might look at Max Lerner, *The Mind and Faith of Justice Holmes: His Speeches, Essays, Letters and Judicial Opinions* (Transaction Publishers, 1989), and Sheldon M. Novick, ed., *Collected Works of Justice Holmes: Complete Public Writings and Selected Judicial Opinions* (University of Chicago Press, 1995), as well as H. L. Pohlman, *Justice Oliver Wendell Holmes: Free Speech and the Living Constitution* (New York University Press, 1991); Gerald Gunther, "Learned Hand and the Origins of Modern First Amendment Doctrine: Some Fragments of History," 27 *Stanford Law Review* 719 (1975); and Fred D. Ragan, "Justice Oliver Wendell Holmes, Zechariah Chafee, Jr., and the Clear and Present Danger Test for Free Speech," 58 *Journal of American History* (1971). A good analysis of Holmes and Brandeis's ideas is Samuel J. Konefsky, *The Legacy of Holmes and Brandeis: A Study in the Influence of Ideas* (Macmillan, 1956); another, concentrating on their free speech jurisprudence, is Pnina Lahav, "Holmes and Brandeis: Libertarian and Republic Justifications for Free Speech," 4 *Journal of Law and Politics* 451 (1988). For Brandeis, see Vincent Blasi, "The First Amendment and the Ideal of Civil Courage: The Brandeis Opinion in *Whitney v. California*," 29 *William and Mary Law Review* 653 (1988); Philippa Strum, *Brandeis: Beyond Progressivism* (University Press of Kansas, 1994; and "The Right to Free Speech" in Strum, ed., *Brandeis on Democracy* (University Press of Kansas, 1995). See Everette E. Dennis et al., eds., *Justice Hugo Black and the First Amendment: "No Law' Means No Law"* (Iowa State University Press, 1978), and Tinsley E. Yarbrough, *Mr. Justice Black and His Critics* (Duke University Press, 1988), for that justice's thinking. Brennan's thoughts are found in William J. Brennan, "Foreword," in Larry Gostin, ed., *Civil Liberties in Conflict* (Routledge, 1988), pp. viii–ix, and "Address at Georgetown University," in *The Great Debate: Interpreting Our Written Constitution* (Federalist Society, 1986), and are discussed in Robert D. Richards, *Uninhibited, Robust, and Wide Open: Mr. Justice Brennan's Legacy to the First Amendment* (Parkway Publishers, 1994).

Anyone interested in the Skokie situation should read Aryeh Neier's *Defending My Enemy* (E. P. Dutton, 1979). Accounts by the Illinois ACLU executive director at the time are in David Hamlin, *The Nazi/Skokie Conflict: A Civil Liberties Battle* (Beacon Press, 1980), and "Swastikas and Survivors: Inside the Skokie-Nazi Free Speech Case," 4 *Civil Liberties Review* 8 (March/April 1978). Other analyses include Franklin S. Haiman, "Nazis in Skokie: Anatomy of the Heckler's Veto," 1978 *Free Speech Yearbook* 11 (1978), written by the Illinois ACLU's former president, and Norman Dorsen, "Is There a Right to Stop Offensive Speech?" in Larry Gostin, ed., *Civil Liberties in Conflict* (Routledge, 1988). Among David Goldberger's articles about the case and related issues are his "Skokie: The First Amendment Under Attack by Its Friends," 29 *Mercer Law Review* 761 (1978); "Lawyers Must Take Even Repugnant Cases," op-ed article, *Los Angeles Times,* April 9, 1978; "The 'Right to Counsel' in Political Cases: The Bar's Failure," 43 *Law and Contemporary Problems* 321 (1979); and "Sources of Judicial Reluctance to Use Psychic Harm as a Basis for Suppressing Racist, Sexist and Ethnically Offensive Speech," 56 *Brooklyn Law Review* 1165 (1991).

The Skokie situation is viewed through the eyes of the survivors in Donald A. Downs, *Nazis in Skokie: Freedom, Community, and the First Amendment* (University of Notre Dame Press, 1985), who makes an argument that he has since rejected for suppression of hate speech. Some of the articles about the case, the ACLU, and approaches to free speech are David G. Barnum, "Decision Making in a Constitutional Democracy: Policy Formation in the Skokie Free Speech Controversy," 44 *Journal of Politics* 480 (1982); James L. Gibson and Richard D. Bingham, "Skokie, Nazis and the Elitist Theory of Democracy," 37 *Western Political Quarterly* 32 (1984); Irving Louis Horowitz and Victoria Curtis Bramson, "Skokie, the ACLU and the Endurance of Democratic Theory," 43 *Law and Contemporary Problems* (Spring 1979); and Carl Cohen, "The Right to be Offensive," *The Nation,* April 15, 1978. Two journalists who commented at the time of the Skokie case are Jim Mann, "Hard Times for the ACLU," *New Republic,* April 15, 1978, and Anthony Lukas, "The A.C.L.U. against Itself," *New York Times Magazine,* July 9, 1978. Theodore R. Mann's speech for the American Jewish Congress is in "Nazis and the First Amendment," 45 *Congress Monthly* (February 1978). Douglas Kneeland wrote about Nazi parties in the United States in "Nazis in U.S.: Small Bands at War with One Another," *New York Times,* April 19, 1978.

Those interested in other studies of speech cases in the United States should look at Richard Polenberg, *Fighting Faiths: The Abrams Case, the Supreme Court, and Free Speech* (1987), and Anthony Lewis, *Make No Law: The Sullivan Case and the First Amendment* (Random House, 1991). On the *Times* case, also see Rodney Smolla, *Suing the Press for Libel: The Media and Power* (Oxford University Press, 1986).

The starting place for information about the ACLU is Samuel Walker, *In Defense of American Liberties: A History of the ACLU* (Oxford University Press, 1990), and Walker, *The American Civil Liberties Union: An Annotated Bibliography* (Garland Publishing, 1992). The Kovno ghetto as experienced by Sol Goldstein and others is the subject of Avraham Tory, ed., *Surviving the Holocaust: The Kovno Ghetto Diary* (Harvard University Press, 1990).

INDEX